The Lost Teachings of Lama Govinda

Lama Govinda and Li Gotami

The Lost Teachings of Lama Govinda

Living Wisdom *from a* Modern Tibetan Master

Richard Power, Editor
Foreword by Lama Surya Das

QUEST

BOOKS

THEOSOPHICAL PUBLISHING HOUSE

Wheaton, Illinois * Chennai, India

Quest Books
Theosophical Publishing House
P.O. Box 270
Wheaton, IL 60189-0270

www.questbooks.net

Cover design, book design, and typesetting by Kirsten Hansen Pott

Photo on page ii courtesy of the Human Dimensions Institute.

LIBRARY OF CONGRESS CATALOGING-IN-PUBLICATION DATA

Govinda, Anagarika Brahmacari.
The lost teachings of Lama Govinda: living wisdom from a modern Tibetan master / edited by Richard Power.
        p.   cm.
Includes bibliographical references and index.
ISBN-13: 978-0-8356-0854-1
ISBN-10: 0-8356-0854-9
1. Spiritual life—Buddhism.   I. Power, Richard, 1953–   II. Title.
BQ4302.G68 2007
294.3'420423—dc22   2007016115

5   4   3   2   1   *   07   08   09   10   11   12

Printed in the United States of America

Contents

Ground Breaking, Bridge Building

by Lama Surya Das

Lama Govinda's was a name I first heard when I was in college in the late 1960s from either Baba Ram Dass, Allen Ginsberg, or Gary Snyder, all of whom had already met him in India. I immediately bought his autobiographical *The Way of the White Clouds,* a spiritual account of his trailblazing 1930s and '40s Tibetan pilgrimages, which helped set me upon a similar journey toward what Govinda lovingly called "The Land of the Thousand Buddhas."

I was amazed to find out that the learned and accomplished Lama Anagarika Govinda—whom I mentally put in a class with the famously reclusive Trappist monk Thomas Merton, author of the classic autobiography *The Seven Story Mountain*—was actually a German guy who had fought in Italy during World War I, had been a monk in Ceylon, and was now married to a flamboyant, upper-class Indian artist named Li Gotami. On winter nights in my college dorm in snowy Buffalo, New York, I read his marvelous tales of Tibet and dreamed of likewise meditating at the feet of the enlightened old Tibetan masters, saints, and sages while imbibing their secret teachings.

Devouring with my eyes the strikingly beautiful and mysterious images of Buddha and the sacred temple architecture in the Govindas' photos, as well as some of their colorful paintings and sketches, I too wanted to become a Buddhist and an eventual Buddha, in order to help edify and enlighten and make peace in this volatile world. I struggled with my Brooklyn-bred mouth to pronounce the Sanskrit and Tibetanized mantras I first read in that early book and asked my calculus teacher from India for help. *The White Clouds* led me to Evans-Wentz's *Tibetan Book of the Dead*, Somerset Maugham's *The Razor's Edge*, Hermann Hesse's *Siddhartha*, and René Daumal's *Mount Analogue*, as well as to the significant works of Alan Watts, Joseph Campbell, Huston Smith, and Herbert V. Guenther—the young seeker was off and running.

Two years later I graduated from college and found my way overland through Europe, Istanbul, Iran, and Afghanistan to fabled India, where I met my first lamas: Thubten Yeshe on a hilltop overlooking Nepal's Katmandu Valley and Kalu Rinpoche in Darjeeling, near where Lama Govinda had met his own root guru, Tomo Geshe. In the library above Katmandu I first studied Govinda's seminal *The Foundations of Tibetan Mysticism* and began to think of the learned lama as a genuine "gnostic intermediary" (a term C. G. Jung coined to describe those extraordinary individuals throughout history who bring spiritual fire into this world by translating, transforming, and helping to make timeless mystical truths relevant to contemporary life). It was from this book that I first learned in fascinating detail about the outer and inner meanings of Govinda's favorite mantra, *Oṁ Maṇi Padme Hūṁ*, a resonant mantra I still chant daily.

Through meditation and self-inquiry, Lama Govinda had obviously passed through the eye of the needle, the secret and mysterious center of his soul, and emerged in the transpersonal, transcendent spirit or divine nature of all and the One, the infinite, the void, the

Godhead, reality, truth, and love—or so I thought at the time and wrote in one of the cheap, little red Indian notebooks I toted on the road. He seemed to have translated monastic talk and contemplative practice, and especially the insider language of esoteric Himalayan Buddhism, into a meaningful dialogue with modernity while revealing its universal existential meaning, a feat exceedingly rare at that early date in the coming of Buddhism to the West, even though it is more prevalent now.

In a chai and pie shop on Freak Street in Katmandu, I heard that the author lived in the foothills of Northwest India at Almora, on the famous Crank's Ridge (known for its eccentric ex-patriots) and resolved to visit him there if the opportunity arose. When visa troubles in Nepal drove me out of the Kopan Monastery in June 1972, I made a pilgrimage to meet the Dalai Lama at his Tibetan capital in exile in Dharamsala, India; and, after spending two weeks there, including some inspiring private time with His Holiness and other wonderful Tibetan teachers, I went on to Almora.

Lama Govinda and Li Gotami were away at the time, but I met their house-sitting holy man, Guru-lama, on the ridge beyond Almora where the Govindas' house had become a sort of informal ashram. Night after night, Guru-lama regaled me with stories around the old fashioned hearth. I slept in my sleeping bag on the small, screened-in porch attached to an acquaintance's rented hill-side house, only slightly in terror of the man-eating tiger rumored to be at large in those hills. I dreamed of the Dalai, of Buddha, of the female Buddha, Tara, and of my Jewish parents in far-off New York. I met an old British relic named Shunya who had known the great saint Ramana Maharshi in the South and fancied himself a sage, although I had my doubts.

R. D. Laing, Ralph Metzner, Richard Alpert (Ram Dass), and Timothy Leary had also spent some time on Crank's Ridge. Indeed, that is where Leary and friends wrote their stoned version of the

Tibetan classic on conscious death, dying, and the afterlife entitled *The Psychedelic Experience: A Manual Based on the Tibetan Book of the Dead*. Concerning the *bardo* passage between lives and other mystical experiences and secret teachings on the sacred nature of mind, it is a book aptly named and reminiscent of William James' classic, *The Varieties of Religious Experience*. Metzner later wrote his own interesting book, *The Varieties of Psychedelic Experience*. It was around that time that, near the feet of our guru, Neem Karoli Baba, I got to know and live with Baba Ram Dass, Bhagavan Das, Krishna Das, Harinam Das, Dan Goleman and Dhamma Dipo, Mirabai Bush, Joseph Goldstein, Sharon Salzberg, and Girija and Larry Brilliant—all slightly older, quite learned, and hip American pilgrims along the same path.

We were all studying and practicing Vipassana meditation and various yogas in those halcyon days, seeking out with our guru's active encouragement the various famous saints of India—Ananda Mayee Ma, Swami Muktananda, Sai Baba, Papa Ram Dass, Gyalwa Karmapa, and so forth. It was a lively and loving *satsang*, an openminded, diverse, and inclusive international ashram community of true brotherhood and sisterhood. There Neem Karoli Baba taught and demonstrated daily how to see the divine in everyone and everything and how to carry such a sacred outlook home with us by learning to love unconditionally, beyond the polar dichotomies of mere personal like and dislike.

I mention these fellow seekers and Bodhisattvas with the warmest memories and gratitude, recalling their kindness to the naive, twenty-one-year-old I was then, just a budding sprout wandering alone on the Buddhist way of rightful living, self-realization, and ultimate awakening. A number of them had been with Lama Govinda himself at his hermitage above Almora. In fact, I doubt there is a single influential American from the early wave of the Dharma's movement to the Western world who had not read and been inspired by Lama Govinda: his life, writings, teachings, and modest and quiet demeanor; and his graceful, dignified person.

From Almora I went further into the mountains to an even smaller village named Kosani, where I stayed at the purely ascetic and sublimely peaceful Gandhi Ashram, with its gorgeous view of the ivory Himalayas arrayed like enormous teeth upon the northern horizon. There each morning for breakfast I drank warm goat's milk right from the bucket, while continuing to read Govinda's and Evans-Wentz's writings and translations, which were important influences on all of us in the present Dharma generation of Hindus and Buddhists, yogis and meditators, and devotees, chanters, spiritual activists, and vegetarians. In one of Govinda's early books, *Psycho-Cosmic Symbolism of the Buddhist Stupa,* I read about stupas (traditional Buddhist reliquary monuments, which took the form of the pagodas so prevalent in Eastern Asia) and wondered how actually to build one in America as part of a contemplative garden and nature sanctuary. This was in 1972. Since then, the idea has taken firm root. Last month I visited the mother of all stupas in the West, Chogyam Trungpa Rinpoche's blessed and splendid Great Dharmakaya Stupa at the Shambhala Mountain Center in the Rockies outside Fort Collins, Colorado.

Rarely a day passes now that I don't think about Lama Govinda. When my friend John White, a spiritual author who happens to be this book's literary agent, asked if I could contribute something to it about Lama Govinda and his fortunately not-lost works, I was delighted. Spirit-sack that I am, I almost cried remembering that marvelous, unexpectedly grace-filled earlier part of my life, feeling my way back into the innocent and earnest spiritual seeker I had been at the time. How much Lama Govinda and all who sailed on his great vehicle did for me and for all of us still being carried along in his uplifting wake! He himself embodied the Bodhisattva Code, the heart-and-soul ideal of the *Mahayana*—the Big boat of universal deliverance that recognizes our kinship with all beings and knows that we all rise and fall, sink or swim together—the realization of which naturally gives birth to empathy, compassion in action, altruism, patience, and loving-kindness. We who are indebted to him in so many ways remain behind like dingies or outriggers being pulled along in the right and true direction even now by the continuously coursing energy of his pioneering efforts.

Lama Govinda was the first Western lama, well accepted and respected by Tibetans during his lifetime. He introduced foremost world-religions scholar Huston Smith to Tibetan Buddhism, which was significantly missing from Smith's groundbreaking contribution to spiritual literacy in the 1950s called *The Religions of Man*, still studied today in universities around the world. Smith went on to record early images of exiled Buddhist monks in the foothills of the Himalayas during the Tibetan diaspora soon after the Chinese takeover of their country in 1959. The result was his classic documentary film, *Requiem for a Faith*, which I highly recommend and show occasionally to my own students. (The film is available from Hartley Film Foundation at http://hartleyfoundation.org.)

Govinda played a vital role in increasing our spiritual literacy and authentic "higher education" here in the West. Through his writings, teachings, and travels, he preserved and disseminated Tibetan Buddhist knowledge in particular—its wisdom, art, iconography, and contemplative practices—along with Eastern thought in general to the modern world long before most of the well-known pioneers had been active in America: Suzuki Roshi, Tarthang Tulku, Chogyam Trungpa, Swami Satchidananda, Maharishi Mahesh Yogi, Ram Dass, and so forth. One of his soul mates, although they probably never met, was the erudite Japanese writer D. T. Suzuki, author of ninety-five books about Zen Buddhism in English. Like Suzuki's, Govinda's many decades of multi-leveled, transectarian scholarship stemmed directly from his own meditational experience and pilgrimages, combined with study and teachings from authentic lineage masters. He helped dispel various misunderstandings about Tibetan Buddhism and set a new standard for modern Buddhists and scholar-practitioners who had previously been forced to rely mainly upon the early Christian missionary dictionaries and translations, the Theosophists' vocabulary, and other affected versions of Buddhist texts by experimental, half-informed, less-experienced authors (such as popularizers Alan Watts, Jack Kerouac, Alexandra David-Neel, and W. Y. Evans-Wentz). Many in the Western world know about Himalayan wisdom principally from glamorized bestsellers that captured the Western imagination, including Lobsang Rampa's *The Third Eye*, James Hilton's *Lost Horizon*—which introduced Americans to the legend of the Himalayan utopian kingdom and remote hidden valley of Shangri-la—and other fantasists. Most of us consider Lama Govinda's work a watershed and turning point for the study and practice of Tibetan Buddhism in the West today, and his well-rounded and fascinating life an inspirational example and Bodhisattva role model for us all. Professor Robert Thurman of Columbia University, a leading authority on Tibet and one of the best and brightest himself, calls Govinda "undoubtedly one of the West's greatest minds, comparable to any of the great geniuses of our century."

I consider Lama Govinda a Second Axial Age personality, a trailblazer not unlike the ancient founders of world religions and the later thinkers in Western Europe's Age of Enlightenment who "laid the spiritual foundations upon which humanity still subsists," to quote German philosopher Karl Jaspers. Govinda contributed mightily to translating Tibetan Buddhism out of the clutches of the ill-termed "Lamaism"—as it was coined by missionaries including Major L. A. Waddell—and its cultish associations with magic, superstition, and ritual. It is largely through Govinda's efforts that the religion is now understood within the more intellectually sound, modern atmosphere of practical wisdom, philosophy and epistemology, meditation and mindful living, mental cultivation and attitude transformation, psychotherapy, neuroscience, and integral healing and socially conscience activism where it is appropriately situated today. If one mistakenly thinks that these somewhat esoteric spiritual interests are merely a faddish fringe or marginal countercultural movement, consider that reputable current polls tell us that thirty to forty million Americans are now practicing meditation or yoga and that approximately 30 percent of Americans believe in reincarnation. There are several thousand registered Buddhist meditation centers in North America and countless yoga studios, centers, and classes, even in health spas and YMCAs. Meanwhile, modern neuroscientific research is benefiting from the knowledge, insights, and practical experience of contemporary meditators and yogis; and the Dalai Lama of Tibet is not just a Nobel Peace Prize Laureate but is also receiving the Congressional Gold Medal, our nation's highest nonmilitary honor, from Congress and the Senate in October of this year in recognition of his contributions to humanity.

As early bridge builders and spiritual pioneers, Lama Govinda and Li Gotami were among the first wave of Dharma teachers coming from the old East who helped open up and bring into being an authentically modern way of following the ancient yet timeless path of awakened enlightenment through the righteous living laid out by the historical Buddha Gautama. They managed to avoid the pitfalls of many spiritual leaders today, including falling prey to empire building, gathering a cultic following, or believing in their own publicity. They made lasting friends wherever they went, free from isolationism, sectarianism, spiritual materialism, narcissism and self-indulgence, commercialism, addiction, opportunism, or scandal. For the Govindas, the sacred Dharma of wise living and inner fulfillment was simply their life, beyond the need for fanfare. They knew who they were and what they were doing and why, and they were free from the need for commercial success. Both were artists as well as global citizens who transcended art and used it to refine consciousness and go beyond themselves. Theirs is a fine model of creative living for us who would follow in their large footsteps.

Fortunately for all of us, this book is based on the Lama's late-life lectures to Western students, bridging the gap between East and West, old and new, the ancient world and modernity, in a relevant, timely, and meaningful fashion. As a transsectarian intellect and global citizen, his expression of perennial wisdom was far beyond the hackneyed and archaic language and mythology of some religionists and the narrow dogmatism of true believers and fanatical new converts. He was a true student of truth and reality, and he loved to learn from new ideas, places, and experiences. Moreover, he could relate easily to people of all kinds, right where they are. This is the kind of "gift of tongues" to which I personally aspire.

In the 1970s, Govinda and Li Gotami met Jeanne Rindge, who founded the well-known Human Dimensions Institute with her husband Fritz in 1961 in upstate New York. (It has now been relocated to Waynesville, North Carolina, where Jeanne resides in her advanced age.) At Jeanne's request, Lama Govinda gave several seminars over the years. He also asked her to help get some of his writings published and gave her, among other things, the essays you now hold in your hand. I'm grateful for the role that Jeanne and the HDI played in helping bring Lama Govinda and Li Gotami to a wider audience again here in the West.

Lama Govinda ended his productive life cared for by his devoted wife, along with students from the San Francisco Zen Center and disciples, near the home of Yvonne Rand in Marin County, California—a house-and-garden sanctuary close to Muir Beach that is now a Buddhist temple and meditation center. Yvonne writes:

I was at Lama and Li's house the night Lama died. We were having dinner: their favorite cheese-and-garlic pizza with Coca-Cola. Suddenly Lama wheeled his chair to the front door and opened it. Then he stood up and died a moment afterward. Only years later, after I had received training in a Vajrayana practice called 'Powa,' did it occur to me that he had long been engaged in that consciousness-transference practice. That's what he must have been doing at the moment he realized what was happening to him.

Occasionally I wonder what he went on to after breathing his last in that lovely Buddha-field by the Bay, where the fog drapes across the Marin Headlands like the white silk scarves the Tibetans drape around the shoulders of statues, pilgrims, and fellow travelers. Sometimes I think I glimpse Lama in the avidly earnest, shining eyes of my youthful students, the Dharma-farmers and future Buddhas of America. He always remains part of the invisible array of ascendant sangha members and lineage holders who guide and accompany us all along the Way.

Lama Surya Das
Dzogchen Center
Cambridge, Massachusetts
May Day 2007

Within the White Cloud:
Life and Work of Lama Govinda

Just as a white summer-cloud, in harmony with heaven and
earth, freely floats in the blue sky from horizon to horizon,
following the breath of the atmosphere—in the same way
the pilgrim abandons himself to the breath of the greater life
that wells up from the depth of his being and leads him beyond
the farthest horizons to an aim which is already present
within him, though yet hidden from his sight.
—Lama Govinda, *The Way of the White Clouds*[1]

Over two thousand five hundred years have passed since the Buddha Shakyamuni turned the Wheel of the Dharma in the Deer Park at Sarnath. For centuries, the teachings spread throughout Asia, evolving into many distinct traditions in India, Southeast Asia, China, Korea, Japan, Tibet, and elsewhere. In the last several decades, facilitated by mass communication, jet-age travel, globalization, and the World Wide Web, the Buddha Dharma has become a planetary force. This dynamic process has been further enriched by the diaspora of the Tibetan people, as well as the westward migration of many other Asian ethnic groups.

The story of how all of this happened is compelling and has many dimensions. The life and work of Lama Anagarika Govinda and his wife, Li Gotami, are inextricably woven into multiple dimensions of that story.

Over thirteen hundred years have passed since Padmasambhava, the Precious Guru, prophesized that "when the iron bird flies and the horses run on wheels, the Tibetan people will be scattered like ants across the world, and the Dharma will come to the land of the red men."[2] In 1959, the Dalai Lama fled Tibet, fulfilling that prophecy. To underscore the poignancy of the prophecy's fulfillment, the Dalai Lama met with three Hopi elders on his first tour of North America in 1979. One of them, Grandfather David, said, "Welcome home."

Of course, although dramatic, profoundly inspiring, and of sweeping cultural and geopolitical importance, the Dalai Lama's journey into exile was not the first visit of a Dharma emissary to the West. The great Japanese Zen abbot Soyen Shaku, the Sri Lankan Buddhist leader Anagarika Dharmapala, and others traveled to the United States for the World Parliament of Religions in 1893.[3] And in the 1960s and 1970s, numerous Buddhist teachers from Tibet (e.g, Chögyam Trungpa), Korea (Dr. Seo), Japan (Suzuki-roshi), Burma and India (Rina Sircar), and elsewhere arrived in the West.

But the story is even richer and more intricately woven, for it is cross-threaded with all those Western seekers—from Theosophical Society founders H. P. Blavastky and Colonel H. S. Olcott to rogue authors, scholars, and artists like W. Y. Evans-Wentz, Nicholas Roerich, Alexandra David-Neel, and yes, the man who would come to be known as Lama Govinda. Overcoming peril and personal hardships, these brave men and women brought the Eastern wisdom back to a parched spiritual landscape.

The triumphs and trials of many beings, known and unknown, from both the East and the West, have established the Buddha Dharma as a planetary force. The echoes of many heartbeats can be heard within deep meditation on the Buddha Dharma. Each one of those heartbeats was a "Turning of the Wheel."

In the 1800s, traveling in the Indian Ocean, Soyen Shaku voyaged on deck because he could not afford cabin passage. Exposed to the heat of the sun, the salt wind, and the rain, without bread or water, he sat motionless while swarms of mosquitoes like black clouds descended on him. Their noise was deafening. He reminded himself of the old legends of the great Bodhisattvas who were willing to offer their limbs for the sake of alleviating suffering and spreading the teachings:

> Repeating such thoughts again and again, I took off my cloth and became stark naked. I sat crossed legged upon the deck, then hurried into the Samadhi which the scriptures call "the Waveless Great Sea." In the beginning I still noticed the hum of the mosquitoes, but as time advanced, I forgot the heat, the hunger and thirst, and at last forgot the mosquitoes.[4]

In March 1959, Tibetans were massing outside the palace in Lhasa chanting, "The Chinese must go! Leave Tibet to the Tibetans!" The Red Army fired mortar rounds and "invited" the young Dalai Lama to an army post three kilometers away. Instead the Dalai Lama took off his maroon monk's robes, donned the garb of a Tibetan soldier with a fur cap on his head and a rifle slung over his shoulder, and trekked with thirty-seven companions across the Himalayas for thirteen days to India.[5]

These anecdotes of courage and equanimity have numerous parallels in the adventures of Westerners like Lama Govinda. He and Li Gotami, like the Dalai Lama, though the Red Army was not pursuing them, had to traverse the Himalayas under most unfavorable circumstances. In the late 1940s, struggling to record as much as they could at the ruins of the ancient city of Tsaparang, Govinda and Gotami stayed too long. They had to fold their "frozen tents with numb fingers," and Govinda had to "break the icicles from his beard." The two passes that offered the best routes out were blocked by heavy snows, so they had to take the much more dangerous option of walking down the course of a frozen river:

> Engaging a crowd of twenty villagers to carry everything, the Govindas set off for the gorge, an extremely deep (several thousand feet) and narrow defile that off-season provided no room for trails. . . . Their descent into the Langchen-Khambab gorge down a series of sand-falls was abrupt and irrevocable. "We had to sit and slip down the hillside to the river's bank," Li explained. . . . Slipping and slithering, they slowly managed the watercourse. At times the ice was too thin, they took to the hillsides, a dangerous situation since they were often sheer. But Li's descriptions of the ice during these times makes the side trips understandable. "Here and there sudden and terrifying gaps appeared in the ice, down which we saw the dark, swirling, swiftly flowing waters. . . ." Boulders also crashed down among them without warning.[6]

And, like Soyen Shaku, Govinda and Li Gotami had some difficult sea voyages, as Govinda relates in this late 1960s' letter from Burma to his friend Bob Shapiro, a Chicago businessman:

> You would probably think that we had reached Calcutta by now, but nothing of the sort! We turned East again and went to Rangoon instead. The heat here is almost unbearable. And since our Java Mail [the ship they had passage on] is not air-conditioned, it is impossible to be in the cabin even for a few minutes, and

we are compelled to sleep on deck, shifting from one corner to another in order to get a little fresh air. One day after Singapore, the kitchen burned out (due to an electrical fire), and for about 10 days no warm meals could be served. In Madras, we had to eat in restaurants in the city and everybody got diarrhea. So we gave up eating altogether. Only now we begin to recover.[7]

Even today, early in the twenty-first century, the saga of Lama Govinda is rich in lessons and inspiration, which glisten with a magical newness and crackle with a crisp relevance.

In his introduction to the 2005 republication of Govinda's autobiographical *The Way of the White Clouds*, Robert Thurman of Columbia University, a distinguished Buddhist scholar in his own right, ranks Govinda as "one of the West's greatest minds of the twentieth century" and equates him with "Einstein, Heisenberg, Wittgenstein, Solzhenitsyn, Gandhi and the Dalai Lama."[8]

Consider this introduction one thread in a celebration of Govinda's extraordinary life and work.

COMPASS READINGS

Very little has been written about the life of Lama Govinda. Although *The Way of the White Clouds* is autobiographical, it concentrates on the narrative of Govinda's journeys in the East, and its insights into other aspects of his life are parenthetical. Almost everything we know about his early life, and much of what we know about his later years, we owe to Ken Winkler and his *A Thousand Journeys: The Biography of Lama Anagarika Govinda*.

Here is a brief narrative woven together from various sources, including the archives of the Human Dimensions Institute, the San Francisco lodge of the Theosophical Society, Winkler's biography, and Govinda's own writings. The timeline reveals three great movements in Govinda's life: the first movement was an *away from* and *toward*, the second movement was an *inward* and *upward*, the third movement was *outward* and *outpouring*. These three movements can also be related to the compass: the first was southward, the second eastward and northward, and the third westward.

In a powerful way, the life of Govinda was both an archetypal expression of the spiritual path and a global circumambulation.

A REMARKABLE ENCOUNTER

In 1962 Huston Smith, the renowned author of *The Religions of Man*, was on his way back to the United States after a lecture tour of Australian universities. He stopped off in Bangkok, Thailand, to visit another respected writer, John Blofeld, whose *Zen Teachings of Huang Po and Hui Hai* had recently been published. Smith wanted to find out more about Zen and was surprised to learn that Blofeld's personal practice flowed from the Tibetan tradition. By his own admission, Smith knew nothing of the Tibetan teachings: "That the word 'Tibet' does not appear in the index of my *Religions of Man*, published in 1958, shows how much my world has changed since then." He resolved to correct the omission on his next academic leave. Two years later, he wrote Blofeld to ask him where to go, and was referred to two monasteries and to a European expatriate named Lama Govinda.

Smith's journal entries from his October 1964 encounter with Govinda, in the foothills of the Himalayas, offer a wonderful demarcation point for our journey into the life and work of this remarkable man:

At the gate to the Govindas' hermitage, prayer flags fluttering in the strong wind, a sign reads, "Visitors from 4 p.m. to Sunset." The sun had just set, but I was warmly welcomed. Lama Govinda is a small man with an oblong, gray Chinese beard, a round face, and an astonishing twinkle. He speaks excellent English with a German accent. Li Gotami is a highly educated Indian artist of Parsi background. Side by side they sit on cushions facing me across a low table. . . .

Eliade's *Yoga: Immortality and Freedom* was on the table. Govinda said it was a good compendium, but didn't penetrate far into the spirit of its subject. [Heinrich] Zimmer did. How a man who never visited India could enter so fully into its spirit was a miracle. . . .

[Govinda] was interested in my interview with the Dalai Lama and his quizzing me on the possible connection between DNA and transmigration. The word "transmigration" is misleading, for in fact nothing migrates. What is real and does bridge lives is a life-direction. In radio transmission, no substance passes from tower to transistor; merely a pattern of energy.

The relativity of time pertains in the spiritual as well as the physical world. By virtue of it, the continuation of a life-direction in another body need not conform precisely to the sequence in physical time.

The concept of a "tulku" differs from that of an "avatar." An avatar is god become man. A tulku is a man who has shaped his life to make a receptacle for the divine. . . .

ESP cannot be doubted. But if one mind can influence another in space, why not in time? This is the basis for Buddhist "transmigration." My mind in this life influences "my" mind in the next.[9]

Blofeld, too, had his own memorable encounter with Govinda:

I learned that the Tibetans themselves accept him as a lama of high attainment without needing to make the smallest allowance for his being a foreigner! . . . Not areas of right action, nor absolute purity of body, speech and mind can alone produce this unique fruit of spiritual understanding which can be achieved only by one far advanced in the arts of mind control and turning a consciousness inward upon itself; but, once gained it declares itself at sight to all but the spiritually dead. The Lama is so soft spoken and modest that I doubt whether he has the remotest idea of the effect he produces on others. . . . Even his gestures have unconsciously acquired something of that almost ritualistic grace which adds so much to the dignity and charm of well-born Tibetans.[10]

Who was Lama Govinda? How did he come to be waiting there for Huston Smith on that beautiful evening? And what was Lama Govinda? Was he actually a tulku born in the West to break and turn the soil for the transplanting of the Bodhi tree?

LOST GENERATION

The man the world would know as Lama Govinda was born Ernst Lothar Hoffman in 1898 in Waldheim, Germany (old kingdom of Saxony). Not much is known about his parents. When he was three years old, his mother, Lolita, died in childbirth. Ernst and his older brother, Oscar, were raised by their maternal aunt Matilda in a trilingual household, in which Spanish, French, and German were spoken. Ernst was sent to boarding school and developed a strong interest in religion and philosophy. Plato and Schopenhauer were early influences. The youth undertook a study comparing Christianity, Islam, and Buddhism, and although he started off with a bias toward Christianity, he soon realized that Buddhism was his natural path.

Then World War I interrupted. In October 1916, Ernst was sent to the Italian frontlines. Two years later, he was hospitalized in Milan after contracting tuberculosis. After he was discharged, Ernst went to Freiburg, Switzerland, to pursue university studies, but he soon returned to Italy. First, he went to the University of Naples, where he immersed himself in a complete set of the Pali canon, which had been donated by King Chulalongkorn of Siam (now Thailand), and added Thai to his linguistic skills. And then, the young German expatriate moved on to the island of Capri, where he immersed himself in its vibrant art colony.

It is interesting to compare the young Hoffman with those two literary prototypes of the Lost Generation, Jake Barnes in Ernst Hemingway's *The Sun Also Rises* and Larry Darrell in W. Somerset Maugham's *The Razor's Edge*. The men whose fates Hemingway and Maugham immortalized in the characters of Barnes and Darrell had the course of their lives disrupted and the core of meaning within them shattered. The savagery and senselessness of war had undone them and cast them adrift. Hemingway's Barnes sought solace in drinking, fishing, and bullfights; Maugham's Darrell traveled to the East to explore the inner life and find the path to enlightenment.

But Ernst Hoffman wasn't "lost;" he was liberated. He had already chosen to focus on the deeper side of life, and he had already determined that the Eastern path was his path. The period of disillusionment and chaos that followed the war-that-unfortu-nately-wasn't-going-to-end-all-wars simply allowed the young man to walk quietly away from the wreckage of European civilization. If it were not for the circumstances of the Lost Generation, he might not have been able to break free. Perhaps he would have become a university professor or a museum curator, expert in something he had never touched or tasted for himself.

In the Bohemian ambience of post–World War I Capri, Ernst met two people who would play important roles in his life: Anne

Halberstam and Earl Brewster. Anne Halberstam, a widow who had lost her daughter to tuberculosis, operated a photography studio. Ernst went to work for her, and was soon living with her and introducing her to people as his "foster mother." Earl Brewster was a wealthy U.S. expatriate, a successful artist and, like Ernst Hoffman, a sincere Buddhist aspirant. (D. H. Lawrence dubbed Brewster the "Buddha Seeker.")[11] Both Halberstam, who followed Govinda to the East to care for him, and Brewster, who went before them and remained Govinda's friend for life, died in India years later.

During the years that Hoffman lived in Italy, he developed his painting technique, studied Buddhist texts, and researched and surveyed Stone Age structures in Sardinia, Tunisia, Morocco, and Malta. These eclectic interests interacted dynamically within him:

> One day while out walking on the far side of the island, Hoffman discovered a large cave. It was so immense, he declared a cathedral could easily fit inside, and he thought it would be a fine place for them to meditate. "There was nothing before me but the huge expanse of the sea and far below me a small road. . . ." Deep inside he found the ruins of a Mithras cult. . . . "I started to explore deep down inside and tried to find if there were any (other) remainders. There was nothing . . . the place was overrun with creepers . . . the roots hanging down, the candlelight. . . . I painted a picture of it and called it The Entrance to The Inferno."[12]

Even decades later, after all he had seen and accomplished, Govinda would conjure that powerful memory in his conversation with Huston Smith:

> Looking back over the years, I find I advanced most through meditation when I followed my own inner leadings and had no external directives. When I was a young man, I was for a few years on the

Isle of Capri. There was an enormous cave there whose mouth looked out on the sea. I found that setting most inspiring.[13]

HOMELESS MONK

In 1929, with the encouragement of his friend Earl Brewster, Ernst Hoffman moved on to Ceylon and his encounter with destiny. His journey was not without travail. He had to travel to the port of Colombo twice. On his first attempt, he was turned away because he did not have sufficient funds. On his second attempt he was again denied entry over a technicality. Dressed in a linen suit and a sun helmet, he languished for hours in the intense heat as the officials prepared to put him on the next ship back to Europe. Desperate and refusing to leave, he threatened to throw the money he would need for steerage back to Marseilles into the water. Finally, with the assistance of someone Brewster sent to rescue him, he succeeded in escaping the authorities and fleeing into the darkness.

Under the auspices of Nyanatiloka Mahathera, the German-born abbot of the Polgasduwa monastery, Ernst began to delve deeper into the Buddha Dharma. The abbot gave him the name "Govinda" (at his own request). He made a pilgrimage to Burma, during which he donned the yellow-colored robe and became an "anagarika" (homeless monk). Henceforward, he introduced himself as "Anagarika Govinda."

"Govinda" is a sacred name in both the Buddhist and Hindu traditions. For the Buddhists, it is the name of one of Gautama Buddha's disciples; for the Hindus, it is one of the names of Krishna. It means "Lord of the Cows." For Lama Govinda himself, it may have also carried an intense personal meaning: Hermann Hesse's masterpiece *Siddhartha* was published in Germany in 1922; in this allegorical novel, Govinda is the name of Siddhartha's best friend and companion on the path to enlightenment.

In *The Way of the White Clouds*, Govinda elaborated on why he took the name "Anagarika":

> I did so in the conscious pursuance of an aim that allowed me neither to make myself "at home" in the security of a monastic community nor in the comforts of a householder's life. Mine was the way of the Siddhas; the way of the individual experience and responsibility, inspired and supported by the living contact between Guru and Chela through the direct transference of power in the act of initiation.[14]

After his return to Ceylon, a tea plantation owner in the mountainous region around Kandy gave him a small plot of land on which he could build a house (provided he did not destroy any tea plants). During this period, Govinda wrote *The Psychological Attitude of Early Buddhist Philosophy*, his first significant contribution to Buddhist scholarship.

Then he was invited to an international Buddhist conference in Darjeeling, in northeast India.

SOME INEXPLICABLE FORCE

Ironically, as Winkler documents, Govinda saw himself journeying to Darjeeling as a missionary:

> He reported being "encouraged by the idea that here was an opportunity to uphold the purity of the Buddha's teachings, as preserved in Ceylon, and to spread its message in a country

where the Buddha Dharma had degenerated into a system of demon-worship and weird beliefs."[15]

While in Darjeeling Govinda made a trip to the nearby Yi-gah Chö-Ling Monastery outside the village of Ghoom, where a storm that raged for three days left him stranded. His stay there radically changed his view of Buddhism and the nature of his quest: "Some inexplicable force," Govinda wrote in *The Way of the White Clouds*, "seemed to keep me back, and the longer I stayed on in this magic world into which I had dropped by a strange concatenation of circumstances, the more I felt that a hitherto unknown form of reality was revealed to me and that I was on the threshold of a new life."[16] It was at Ghoom that Govinda met his teacher, a powerful and enigmatic man named Tomo Geshe Rinpoche.

Govinda also spent some time in Bengal, teaching at Shantiniketan, Rabindrinath Tagore's international school in Calcutta. One of his favorite students was a willful girl named Indira Nehru, later known to the world as Indira Ghandi, India's first woman prime minister. Govinda taught her French. Another of his students was an alluring young Parsee woman named Rati Petit, an accomplished artist and photographer who would later be known to the world as Li Gotami, Govinda's wife, collaborator, and fellow explorer. During this period, Govinda wrote *Psycho-Cosmic Symbolism of the Buddhist Stupa*.

In the early 1930s, Govinda began his explorations of Tibet; in particular, he visited the Chumbi Valley, Ladahk, and the Chang-Thang. In 1936, Tomo Geshe Rinpoche died.

During World War II, Govinda was interred—for five years. The suspicion generated by his German birth and his friendship with the Nehru family (who were leaders in the Indian independence movement) outweighed his British passport. The two thousand prisoners in the Premnagar camp were separated into two groups, one pro-Nazi, the other anti-Nazi. Govinda aligned himself with the smaller anti-Nazi group. Throughout the ordeal, he and another German, a Theravadin monk named Nyanaponika Mahathera, studied and meditated together.

In 1947, Lama Govinda and Li Gotami were married, four times. There were civil ceremonies in both Bombay and Darjeeling, and "lama marriage" ceremonies performed by Ajo Rinpoche in the Chumbi Valley and by Govinda himself.

SACRED CIRCLE OF HIGHEST BLISS

In July 1948, Govinda and Gotami struck out for the ancient city of Tsaparang in Western Tibet. Li's extraordinary photographic record of the expedition would be preserved for posterity in her book *Tibet in Pictures: A Journey Into the Past*. This trek was also of central importance in Govinda's own *Way of the White Clouds*.

Li Gotami chronicled the journey for the *Illustrated Weekly of India*: "The rain nearly froze us while the wind howled like hungry wolves around us. Oh, those winds! They are Tibet's worst enemies, and if I was ever asked to picture them I would draw a hundred thousand ice-bound daggers with the head of a howling wolf for every hilt."[17]

In September, they reached Tsaparang, a long-deserted city in a desiccated region, and, as Winkler describes, they established themselves there in very harsh circumstances: "Taking shelter in a crude stone hut whose rough interior and sooty walls reminded them of a cave, the Govindas settled in for a long stay. . . . Porridge and chapattis formed their two meals a day, cooked slowly over yak dung and brushwood fires. Tea had to be drunk quickly before it froze in their cups."[18] They toiled for many weeks, deep into December. Building and hanging from scaffolding, always struggling for more light, they painstakingly photographed, sketched, and traced the surviving frescoes, bearing witness to their extraordinary beauty and power.

In the ruins of Tsaparang, Govinda came across a place of both impersonal power and personal revelation that seemed—like his discovery of the Mithraic cult cave on the isle of Capri two decades earlier—to serve as a punctuation point for another significant juncture in his life's journey:

> Moving about as in a dream, in which past and present were interwoven into a fabric of four-dimensional reality, I suddenly stood before the half-open door of an almost completely preserved building, which by some miracle had escaped the general destruction.
>
> With a strange feeling of expectancy I entered into the death-like stillness of a half-dark room, in which the secrets of centuries seemed to be present and to weigh upon me like the fate of an unfulfilled past. When finally my eyes had become accustomed to the darkness, my premonitions became certainty: I stood in the Holy of Holies of a mystery temple, the chamber of initiation, in which the great *mandala*, 'the Sacred Circle of Highest Bliss', (*dPal hKhor-lo bDem-chog*) is revealed before the eyes of the initiate, in all its manifold forms of celestial splendour, divine figures and cosmic symbols.[19]

OTHER TRAILBLAZERS

In his life in India and on his excursions into Tibet, Lama Govinda encountered many other adventurers. Some were fellow seekers, some were opportunists, some were thrill-seekers, and some had hidden agendas. Three of the people he encountered along the way stand out as of particular importance in the early phases of the overall movement to bring word of Tibet's wisdom treasures to the West: Alexandra David-Neel, Heinrich Harrer, and Dr. W. Y. Evans-Wentz.

The Frenchwoman Alexandra David-Neel was an explorer, a Buddhist, a spiritualist, an anarchist, and, like Govinda, the author of more than thirty books, including *Magic and Mystery in Tibet* and *Secret Oral Teachings in Tibetan Buddhist Texts*. She died in 1969 at the age of one hundred.

The German mountain climber, Olympic skier, and SS member Heinrich Harrer participated in a German expedition into Tibet, escaped from the same British internment camp where Govinda was held, befriended the young Dalai Lama, and wrote *Seven Years in Tibet*, which was translated into fifty-three languages, sold three million copies, and was made into a Hollywood film starring Brad Pitt.

The American scholar, explorer, and spiritual aspirant Dr. W. Y. Evans-Wentz authored four seminal texts for Oxford University Press—*The Tibetan Book of the Dead, Tibet's Great Yogi Milarepa, Tibetan Yoga and Secret Doctrine*, and *The Tibetan Book of the Great Liberation*—and could count Carl Jung among those whose work he influenced directly. Evans-Wentz became one of the Govindas' benefactors, providing them with a home on Kesar Devi ridge in Almora in northern India, an act of generosity that made a profound difference in the lives of Lama Govinda and Li Gotami in the 1950s:

> It was a turning point in Lama Govinda's life. No more would he have to deal with the hustle and bustle of the plains or be concerned about inadequate quarters and capricious landlords. Li Gotami felt they were being offered a refuge, an act, in her eyes, of extreme sanctity. As a Parsee, a member of a community who had taken refuge in India for hundreds of years, she considered such a gesture to be of the highest order. It proved to be their most productive period.[20]

In his notes on their 1962 conversations, Huston Smith record-ed some of Govinda's candid insights on David-Neel, Harrer, and other trailblazers:

> Mrs. David-Neel's *Mysticism and Magic in Tibet* is 99% true. The only point he doubts is that she projected figures as she claims. She is a bit cynical (she's from a Huguenot, anti-ritual background) and has a journalist's interest in the bizarre. Nevertheless, she's good.
>
> Arthur Avalon: Sincere, genuinely religious, and reliable except when he writes on Buddhism. But single-handed he rescued Hindu tantra from slander. . . .
>
> Heinrich Harrar's *Seven Years in Tibet* makes no pretense of being interested in religion, but on the aspects of life about which he writes it's all right.
>
> Superficial as the book may be in many respects, James Hilton's *Lost Horizons* contains a profound simile. When the residents of Shangri-la crossed the mountains from Tibet, their youth faded and they become old at once. So it must be, alas, with Tibetan Buddhism. An entire field is needed to sustain such spiritual intensity and feats. The only hope is that somewhere in the mountains—Tibet is large—there are hermit saints who, if the occupation passes within a generation, can then reconstitute the faith."[21]

Beat and Hippie Generations

The arc of Lama Govinda's life, so rich in spiritual questing and geographical exploration, tracks with the whole cultural arc of mid-twentieth-century history from the Lost Generation of the 1920s and 1930s to the Beatnik era of the 1950s and the Hippie scene of the 1960s.

Foundations of Tibetan Mysticism was published in 1960. In 1961, Gary Snyder and Allen Ginsberg visited Lama Govinda in Almora. "He said Allen Ginsberg has visited him and left him a volume of his poetry," Huston Smith wrote in his notes. "Sweet of him, but Govinda had to write and say he didn't get what he was after. One could see a certain craftsmanship in his work, but why would one want to pour out that kind of stuff? Still, there is vitality in such men, and one is always glad to see life."[22]

In 1962, China invaded India. Lama Govinda returned to Europe after a thirty-year absence, first as a guest of the Italian government and then, in 1965, at the invitation of Arya Maitreya Mandala (AMM), the organization Govinda had started with Tomo Geshe Rinpoche.

In 1966, *The Way of the White Clouds* was published. Commercial jets and mass communication had made the world much more intimate. Infused by the diaspora of the Tibetans and popularized by writers such as Jack Kerouac, Alan Watts, and Ram Dass, as well as Snyder and Ginsberg, Eastern religion in general and Buddhism in particular exploded in the consciousness of the West. The Beatles traveled to India in search of a deeper vision of reality, and so did those influenced by their music.

THE VAJRA OF THE HEART

Many ardent seekers and dedicated workers in the West reached out to Govinda during the halcyon days of the late 1960s and early 1970s. They included several individuals in San Francisco, California, which was, of course, one of the hotbeds of the West's revolution in consciousness.

Some letters from Govinda found in the archives of the San Francisco lodge of the Theosophical Society offer precious glimpses into this period. Joe and Guin Miller, two American Theosophists, had an intimate spiritual friendship with W. Y. Evans-Wentz, and were to become legendary in their own right for leading hundreds of young people in "walking meditations" through Golden Gate Park. (Evans-Wentz considered Joe Miller "the only person to understand the theories on the Clear Light of Reality,"[23] one of the obscure texts included in his *Tibetan Yoga and Secret Doctrines*.)

In an August 16, 1967, letter to the Millers, Govinda wrote of his hopes for the West:

> What the West (Europe as well as America) needs, are centres of meditation, in which man can find himself again. For this nothing else is required but the quietness of nature and the stillness of the mind. It is there that the East and West shall meet, and the Vajra of the Heart shall be realized.[24]

Govinda's reference to "the Vajra of the Heart" is an acknowledgment of the personal friendship with and devotion to Dr. Evans-Wentz that served as a bond between Govinda, Gotami, and the Millers. It is a prayer at the conclusion of the Doctrine of the Long Hum, a short text included in Evans-Wentz's *Tibetan Yoga and Secret Doctrine*.

In his own oral history, Joe Miller explains the meaning of the phrase:

> In the Long Hum, it says, "May the Vajra of the Heart be realized in this lifetime." And do you know what Vajra means? Heart, the diamond of the heart. And the diamond, when it is polished, can reflect any facet or color in existence. And it's the hardest gem. We can even use it to make drills that bore down

through a rock. So when you're having a tough time and life is giving you hell, then you know the Divine Lapidary is just polishing another jewel of consciousness.[25]

In an October 22, 1967, letter to Dr. Adjari Warwick, an enigmatic personality who dressed commando-style with a red beret, knapsack, and hiking gear, and presented himself as an officer in the "Tibetan medical corps"[26] and whom Govinda gave the initiation name "Vajrabodhi," the Lama wrote of the mission of the AMM and of the future:

> I had the good fortune to receive initiation by Gurus representing all three major Schools of Tibetan Buddhism, resulting in the foundation of the first international Vajrayāna Order, the Arya Maitreya Mandala which strives to unite the complete Buddhist tradition, culminating in the Vajrayāna and thus looking forward to the coming Buddha Maitreya. . . . His emblem is the Double Vajra, signifying not only universality, but the realization of the Fourth Dimension, the Vajrakāya, the synthesis of the Three Bodies (Dharmakāya, Sambhogakāya, Nirmāṇakāya). . . . I am relieved to see that a younger generation is taking over the work to organize the young Buddhist movement in various countries. I am in my 70th year and my forces are limited, but I will do my best to help and to advise you and all those who sincerely wish to pursue the Bodhisattva Way and the universal teachings of the Vajrayāna.[27]

In a February 15, 1968, letter to "Vajrabodhi," Govinda offered some cautionary insights on the challenges of establishing an entity such as his AMM in the West:

In one of your letters . . . you say that in Europe—and in Germany especially—we were dealing with individuals, "but in America, England and Hawaii we are dealing with corporations, and spiritual/clerical combines of some years standing." This is a complete misunderstanding. An Order, such as the AMM, only deals with individuals, never with corporations or organizations as a whole, though we may cooperate with them. Our Order is based on personal relationship between each Member and the Line of the Gurus, who have transmitted the living power of the Dharma. . . . Our Order represents a spiritual hierarchy—not a democratic society, in which heads are counted irrespective of what is in them. . . . A 'Mandala' is not a collection of heterogeneous elements, but an organized unity of individuals grouped around and directed toward a common centre, represented by the ideal and the active path of the Vajrayāna, as the integration and culmination of all previous Schools of Buddhism.[28]

In a January 16, 1968, letter to Gene Wagner of the American Buddhist Order (ABO), Govinda pointed out a "small inaccuracy" in an article Wagner had written:

The difference between a Mantra and a Dhāraṇi has nothing to do with whether they are used individually or collectively. A dhāraṇi is generally a combination of mantras. The mantra, thus, is a shorter form of dhāraṇi, while bīja-mantra is the further reduction into a single sound. For example, the mantra OṀ MAṆI PADME HŪṀ can be condensed into the bīja-mantra ("seed-syllable") HRIH! . . . However, more important than all of this is the fact that a mantra has no power unless it has been given by the Guru during initiation, because without initiation and the training that goes before it, the mantra has neither meaning nor power. . . . As to pronunciation, not only vowels are important, but even more so the rhythm, which depends on the accent. . . . If Rev. [Iru] Price brings his tape-recorder when he comes here, I shall recite some of our main mantras for all of you.[29]

IN THE WESTERN PARADISE

In 1968, Govinda and Gotami traveled to America by ship. Their four-month tour took them to New York, Chicago, and several other northeastern and midwestern cities, as well as numerous venues in northern California, including San Francisco and Big Sur; and then they came to rest on Alan Watts's houseboat in Sausalito.

They also picked up Evans-Wentz's ashes to bring them back to Kesar Devi:

> Taking Evans-Wentz's ashes through Indian customs presented a suspenseful moment for the Govindas. They had packed them in their trunk, hopefully at a level the officials would ignore. Lama Govinda told me that he didn't know what their reactions would be. When their turn arrived for luggage inspection, the official in charge took one look at their robes and waved them on.[30]

In 1971, they were traveling again—back to the United States (California, mostly), Canada, Europe, and South Africa. In 1975, after another speaking tour, this one in the Midwest, the Govindas took up residence at Tarthang Tulku's Nyingma Institute in Berkeley, California, and then returned to Alan Watts's houseboat for a few more months. Late in the year, Lama Govinda suffered a stroke.

In the late 1970s, Li Gotami was feeling the effects of Parkinson's disease. The Govindas were invited to live in Mill Valley, California, under the auspices of Richard Baker-roshi's San

Francisco Zen Center. In 1978, Lama Govinda underwent gall
bladder surgery. In 1979, a two-volume edition of *Tibet in Pictures*
was published, and in 1981 Govinda's *Inner Structure of the I
CHING* was published.

On January 15, 1985, Govinda suffered another stroke and
died in his beloved Li Gotami's arms. Several months after Govinda's death, Li Gotami returned to India to live with her family.

THE BODY OF GOVINDA'S
GREAT WORKS TELLS A TALE

Govinda wrote prodigiously and taught tirelessly. A comprehensive
and in-depth exploration of his works would be a worthy
undertaking, but the introduction to this collection is not the
appropriate vehicle for it. Instead, we will explore themes and
insights from what are arguably Govinda's five most important
books: *The Way of the White Clouds*; *Foundations of Tibetan
Mysticism*; *Psycho-Cosmic Symbolism of the Buddhist Stupa*; *Creative
Meditation and Multi-Dimensional Consciousness*; and *The Inner
Structure of the I CHING*. Taken together, they tell an illuminating
tale of a self-described pilgrim who beheld visions in wild places,
uttered a great mantra, circumambulated holy sites, and had both
his inner and outer perceptions transformed.

Three Visions That Illuminated the Pilgrim's Path

Three visions provide the framework for *The Way of the White
Clouds*: "The Poet's Vision" and "The Guru's Vision" open the first
section of the autobiography, and "The Chela's Vision" closes the
first section.

In the "Poet's Vision," Govinda shares an experience he had
in the ruins of Tsaparang: "The great Red Temple of Buddha

Shakyamuni was filled with darkness and silence. . . . Suddenly a tremor, accompanied by the rumbling sounds of falling masonry, shook the walls of the temple."[31] The window shutters burst open, Govinda reports, and the full moon shone down on the head of Buddha Shakyamuni. He heard "the moaning and groaning of innumerable voices." A big crack had opened up in the wall, next to the White Tara, and in close proximity to one of the flowers that had been placed at the sides of her throne.

Govinda recounts a dialogue between the flower and the White Tara. The "Spirit of Beauty," speaking through the flower, pleads to the White Tara for protection for itself and the sacred site all around it. But Tara, citing the Prajñaparamita Sutra, reminds the flower that the world is but a "flickering lamp" and a fleeting dream.[32] Undaunted, the Spirit of Beauty acknowledges the truth of utter transience and urges another, equally irrefutable truth, the Bodhisattva vow, on the Goddess. He entreats Tara to intercede and save the temple from destruction for the sake of all sentient beings, so that the texts and other treasures could be preserved to awaken the still-slumbering consciousness of the multitudes. His prayer is answered: "Thy wish shall be granted, Spirit of Beauty! Thy form, as well as that of the others inhabiting this temple, shall not perish until their message has been delivered to the world, their sacred purpose fulfilled."[33]

And for good measure, the five Dhyāni Buddhas, also represented by statues in the temple, each stirred, in turn, bestowing blessings and gifts on the place itself and on those present (i.e., Govinda himself, of course).

In the "Guru's Vision," Govinda recounts a legendary experience of his initiator, Tomo Geshe Rinpoche, which occurred at Chorten Nyima, a place sacred to Padmasambhava near the border with Sikkim. Chorten Nyima is a scene of vastness, at one of the highest points on the Tibetan plateau, "a place where heaven and earth meet on equal terms." And against that backdrop of "a dark blue sky," Tomo Geshe Rinpoche beheld the whole pantheon of Buddhas and Bodhisattvas, from all three times, and from every dimension, "dazzling in all the colours of the rainbow."

At first, only the Rinpoche was able to see this vision, but after a while it became so palpable that everyone present could share in it. "Moreover, all the differentiations of mountains and waters and rocks and plants, and all that makes up our common world, blended into one another and faded away, leaving only the indescribable experience of primordial unity—not dull and inert, but vibrant with rhythmic life and light, with celestial sounds of songs and harmonies, melodiously rising and falling and merging and then fading into silence."[34]

In his description of the third vision, the "Chela's Vision," Govinda writes of resting in a monastery after a long day of riding. Over the centuries, the monastery had grown up around the cave of a hermit. As Govinda relaxed in the pre-sunset quietude, he felt "great peace and inner serenity." His attention was drawn to the "irregular surface" of a freshly plastered wall in the room he occupied. Soon, he discerned a landscape emerging as if from the hands of an invisible sculptor who worked from inside the material of the wall itself. From within this landscape, a majestic Buddha appeared. Govinda knew it to be Maitreya, the coming Buddha.

He closed his eyes, and when he opened them again, a wrathful deity had supplanted the beneficent teaching Buddha; "his raised, flame-like hair was adorned with human skulls, his right arm stretched out in a threatening gesture, wielding a diamond sceptre." Rather than being frightened, Govinda "felt the strange beauty in the powerful expression of this terrifying form of Vajrapāni, the defender of truth against the powers of darkness and ignorance, the Master of Unfathomable Mysteries."

Then Manjusri and Tara appeared in succession. Govinda was overcome by the great compassion that exuded from this emanation of Tara. She was, for him, the "liveliest embodiment" of Buddha Shakyamuni's words: "Like a mother, who protects her child, her only child, with her own life, thus one should cultivate a heart of unlimited love and compassion towards all living beings." Her head burst into a thousand heads, her arms split into a thousand arms, her loving hands reached out in all directions. Within each hand was a radiant eye. Then everything dissolved into light, and the vision passed.[35]

In the first vision, Govinda was granted protection for what he had to do; through the second vision, which was his Guru's not his own, Govinda was vouchsafed the reality of the spiritual hierarchy and the oneness of all life; in the third vision, again Govinda's, he was offered a glimpse of humanity's promise and urged on to dedicate all his efforts to the alleviation of human suffering and the liberation of his fellow beings.

What the Pilgrim Whispered

The title Govinda originally intended for the book that came to be known as *Foundations of Tibetan Mysticism* was simply *Oṁ Maṇi Padme Hūṁ*. He was disappointed to discover that there already was a book in print with that title. Nevertheless, *Foundations of Tibetan Mysticism*, which became a standard text for many years, is indeed an exploration of the meaning and power of the six-syllable mantra.

Throughout Tibet, "Oṁ Maṇi Padme Hūṁ" is everywhere—countless prayer flags have it printed on them, countless rocks have it painted on them, countless Dharma wheels have it inscribed on them. Its power is legendary, and its meaning profound.

OṀ: "OṀ is associated with liberation," Govinda writes, either as a means to it, or as a symbol of its attainment. . . . Like a mirror which reflects all forms and colors, without changing its own nature, so OṀ reflects the shades of all temperaments and takes the shapes of all higher ideals, without confining itself exclusively to any one of them. Had this sacred syllable been identified with any conceptual meaning, had it entirely yielded to any particular ideal, without retaining that irrational and intangible quality of its kernel, it would never have been able to symbolize that super-conscious state of mind, in which all individual aspirations find their synthesis and their realization.[36]

MAṆI: In regard to MAṆI, Govinda invoked the words of the Buddha, "There is, O Monks, an Unborn, Unoriginated, Uncreated, Unformed," and suggested that anyone who realizes this has "truly found the Philosopher's Stone, the precious jewel (*maṇi*), the *prima materia* of the human mind, nay, of the very faculty of consciousness in whatever form of life it might appear." Govinda saw it as "the real aim of all great alchemists."[37]

PADME: Just as the lotus grows up from the darkness of the mud to the surface of the water, opening its blossom only after it has raised itself beyond the surface, and remaining unsullied from both earth and water, which nourished it—in the same way the mind, born in the human body, unfolds its true qualities ("petals") after it has raised itself beyond the turbid floods of passions and ignorance, and transforms the dark powers of the depths into the radiantly pure nectar of Enlightenment-consciousness (*bodhi-citta*), the incomparable jewel ("maṇi") in the lotus-blossom ("padma").[38]

HŪM: To understand the meaning and power of HŪM, Govinda asserts, you must come to terms with one particular aspect of Tantric Buddhism, which is "misunderstood even more than all of the other features"—namely, "a class of beings, forces, or symbols, whose nature is closely related to the seed-syllable HŪM, and who appear to the outsider more or less demoniacal." Because these beings "seem to embody all that we cannot fit into our well-ordered thought-world," they "appear to us threatening, dangerous and terrifying." The aspect of knowledge expressed in HŪM "can only be experienced if we transcend the boundaries of thought, as in the ecstatic moment of a flashlike direct insight into the true nature of things or of ourselves, breaking through the tension of our inner being and forcing us to leap into the unknown."[39]

What the Pilgrim Circumambulated

Just as the six-syllable mantra has been invoked wherever Buddha Dharma has flourished, so have stupas been erected, and honored with circumambulation and the offering of incense and flowers. And just as Govinda unlocked the meaning and power of "Oṁ Maṇi Padme Hūṁ" in *Foundations of Tibetan Mysticism,* he unlocks the meaning and power of the monuments in *Psycho-Cosmic Symbolism of the Buddhist Stupa.*

Although the design of stupas evolved differently from one culture to another, and over many centuries, "the original stupas," according to Govinda, "consisted of an almost hemispherical tumulus and an altar-like structure (harmika) on its top, surmounted by one or several superimposed honorific umbrellas."[40]

"The Buddhist universe," Govinda writes,

is the universe of conscious experience. The symbolism of the stupa can be read, therefore, in the cosmic as well as the psychic sense. Its synthesis is the psycho-cosmic image of Man, in which the physical elements and the laws of nature and their spiritual counterparts, the different world-planes and their corresponding stages of consciousness, as well as that which transcends them, have their place. . . . The Nepalese stupas, which in many cases have preserved archaic features, decorate the harmika with painted human eyes, thus suggesting a human figure in the posture of meditation hidden in the stupa, the crossed legs in the base, the body up to the shoulders in the hemisphere, the head in the harmika. This also corresponds to the psycho-physiological doctrine of the centers of psychic force (cakras) which are located in the body and through which consciousness develops.[41]

What the Pilgrim Saw Inside

In *Creative Meditation and Multi-Dimensional Consciousness*, Govinda illuminates the "Basic Elements of Vajrayāna Meditation," articulating the "Four Symphonic Movements of Meditation," which corresponds to four of the Dhyāni Buddhas (meditation or medicine Buddhas).

First Movement

This moment, in which time stands still—because it is empty of all designations of time, space, and movement but is nevertheless a moment of infinite potentialities—represents the state of pure "being" or "isness," which we can only express by the word *śūnyatā*, as indicating the primordial ground from which everything originates. It is the timeless moment before creation or, seen from the standpoint of the individual, the moment of pure receptivity which precedes all creative activity.

It is the first movement in the great symphonic mandala or magic circle, in which our inner world appears as sound and light, color and form, thought and vision, rhythm and harmonious coordination, visible symbol and meditative experience. . . . In the light of this mirror-like wisdom things are freed from their "thingness."[42]

Second Movement

By recognizing our own nature as śūnyatā, we realize that it is not different from the essential nature of all living beings. This is the "Equalizing Wisdom" or "The Wisdom of Equality," in which we turn from the cool and detached attitude of an observer to the warm human feeling of all-embracing compassion for all that lives.[43]

Third Movement

Thus we come to the "third movement" of meditative experience in which we are concerned neither with concrete beings nor with material things. Here both differentiation and unity, form and emptiness, the purity of light and the infinite modulations of color are revealed in their infinite interrelatedness without losing their distinctive qualities and individuality of expression. This is the "Distinguishing Wisdom," in which our mind, our discriminating, judging intellect turns into the intuitive consciousness of inner vision, in which "the special and general characteristics of all things become clearly visible without hindrances."[44]

Fourth Movement

The "fourth movement" of meditative experience belongs to the realm of action and willpower and represents the "All Accomplishing Wisdom," the "Wisdom that Accomplishes All Works." Here volition and its formative tendencies (*samskāra skandha*) are transformed into the selfless, "karma-free" action of a life dedicated to enlightenment, motivated by compassion and based on the understanding of both the individual and the universal aspect of life and phenomena, as experienced in the previous three movements.[45]

What the Pilgrim Saw Outside

In the course of his life's work, Lama Govinda distilled and articulated his own in-depth analysis and experiential approach not only to the Tantric Buddhism of Tibet—the secrets of mantra, mandala, meditation, etc.—but also to the I Ching, the ancient Chinese Taoist text, also known as the Book of Changes, or, as Govinda called it, the Book of Transformation.

At Almora, Govinda told Huston Smith that "the psychology of the I Ching" was "profound" and "differs from that of Buddhism in that it instructs us" on "how to respond to the world as it currently presents itself," whereas Buddhism "wants to change the world as experienced."[46]

In *The Inner Structure of the I CHING*, Govinda wrote that the ancient text offers a pathway to opening the inner eye to a second level of reality:

In fact, the more we observe the laws of the world and of our own thinking, feeling and experiencing, the more we shall become aware that what we call reality operates on two levels or in two directions. The first proceeds horizontally and corresponds to the law of cause and effect on which our logic is based; the other may be called the law of synchronicity. While the first proceeds in time, and more or less in a straight line of successive events which condition each other (logic), the second connects events that occur simultaneously, without logical connection, but for reasons that are beyond our understanding and observation. This second level of reality connects events that are not subject to our time-sense, and can therefore not be associated with our horizontal line of successive events in time, but with lines that stand perpendicular to our assumed time-line. The connections belong to the world of our intuition, rising up from the dark abyss of our inner being, in which cosmic laws find their individual expression.[47]

LOST TEACHINGS

The Lost Teachings of Lama Govinda: Living Wisdom from a Modern Tibetan Master is a celebration of a life and work of importance to the future of both the East and the West. A casual reader might see the importance and relevance of Govinda's contribution at an end. After all, the Tibetan tradition, like numerous other strains of Eastern wisdom, has been established in the West. Many earnest lamas and great rinpoches have performed empowerments, led retreats, and built centers in Europe and the Americas. Many sacred scriptures and insightful commentaries, once read only by those daring and fortunate enough to trek to the high places, can now be ordered online from Amazon or Barnes and Noble and be delivered within days.

But such a view is seriously flawed. If Govinda's work were simply that of an early scholar and translator of Tibetan teachings, perhaps it would be true. But his work (and the work of Evans-Wentz as well) was more than just that.

The East and the West have evolved along divergent paths, culturally, philosophically, religiously, for many centuries. And indeed, even within the East itself, the Buddha Dharma has evolved along divergent paths from one region to another.

Certainly, all of this diversity, with its richness and its subtleties, has not evolved over so many centuries simply to be subsumed by one side or the other. If the West were simply to embrace the mysticism of the East, or vice versa, it would be a tragic loss for both civilizations. A world culture, a global spice-chest of mysticism, is being forged here in the twenty-first century. What is Western is uniquely Western, what is Eastern remains uniquely Eastern—but in addition, something new, something planetary, is coming into being and consciousness; and men and women like Govinda and Li Gotami served as bridges—not one-way bridges either—to that twenty-first century mysticism.

Composed of several essays provided to Human Dimensions Institute (HDI) in the 1970s and a transcript of dialogues from HDI workshops with Lama Govinda held during that period, the content of *The Lost Teachings of Lama Govinda: Living Wisdom from a Modern Tibetan Master* highlights this global aspect of the Lama's contribution. *Lost Teachings* shows not only that Govinda was ahead of the curve back in the 1960s and 1970s, but also how relevant he is to the current and future dialogue here in the early twenty-first century.

In "From Theravada to Zen," Lama Govinda explores the ways in which the Japanese Zen and Chinese Ch'an traditions reach back to the essential nature of early Buddhist teachings. Instead of highlighting incidental differences and conditional distinctions within the many Buddhist traditions, Govinda emphasizes the central truth of *śūnyatā* (emptiness, voidness) and points toward a global approach to the Buddha Dharma that overcomes relative distinctions and difference:

> Recognizing this experience as the real starting point of Buddhism and not as only a distant, more or less theoretical aim or ideal, the followers of Ch'an Buddhism in China and of Zen in Japan try to go back to the very origin of Buddhist tradition by insisting on the spontaneity of the human mind, which basically

is not different from that of the Buddha, if only we can free it from the cobwebs of habitual thought and prejudice. They maintain that we have to replace book knowledge by direct experience, scholarliness by intuition, and the historical Buddha by the Buddha within us—by awakening the potentialities of our mind, which will lead to the realization of perfect enlightenment. It is a courageous attempt that requires complete self-dedication and complete surrender of one's whole being, without reservations, without holding back anything to which our ego can cling.

In "*The Act of Will* and Its Role in the Practice of Meditation," Lama Govinda explores those dimensions of the psyche where Western psychology and Eastern mysticism intersect, using the work of Roberto Assagioli, a pioneer in the psychoanalytic movement, as a launching point. Assagioli, author of *The Act of Will*, had studied with Sigmund Freud, and was the founder of a form of transpersonal psychology called psychosynthesis. In Assagioli's views on the higher role of the will in human experience, Govinda found common ground:

It is clear that this "will" is not the ego-motivated will of the ordinary self-seeking individual, but what Assagioli would term the "Transpersonal Will," a will that has been sublimated and transformed into a force, directed beyond all narrow aims and purposes, transcending individual limitations, and finally turning the individual into "a willing channel through which the powerful energies of the universe flow and operate."

As long as the individual bars this channel by its ego-directed will, its illusion of separateness, or by simply being unaware of this potential source of energies, it cannot make use of it. Meditational practices have, therefore, no other purpose than to awaken, to develop, and to strengthen the awareness of the individual, to remove the hindrances that stand in the way of the free flow of creative and life-giving energies, to open the mind to the infinite possibilities of experience, and to make it an instrument capable of integrating those experiences in actual life.

In "Teilhard de Chardin in the Mirror of Eastern Thought," Govinda explores the depth of common mystical experience from which both Buddhism and Christianity draw:

Perhaps you are familiar with the mantric formula *Oṁ Maṇi Padme Hūṁ*. It is generally interpreted in a very superficial manner as "the dewdrop in the Lotus," which sounds very poetical but has little to do with the real meaning, as far as this can be expressed in simple words. The mantra expresses that the jewel (mani) of divine reality must be realized in the lotus-like vessel (padma) of our own heart. Teilhard de Chardin says this in a similar way and in almost identical terms: "My chalice and my paten are in the depth of a soul, which is wide open to all forces, which in one moment rise from all points of the earth (world) and converge upon the spirit."

What has happened in these few words is so wonderful that I feel that they could only be those of a man who had gone through an experience of profound vision and clarity of mind. Here we have a definition and a clear picture. The human mind, the whole consciousness, converges towards the spirit, when all forces and qualities of the individual and its surroundings converge toward completeness within it.

In "Drugs and Meditation: Consciousness Expansion and Disintegration versus Concentration and Spiritual Regeneration," Govinda weighed in on the efficacy of using psychedelics as a spiritual tool, on behalf of which proponents such as Timothy Leary in Go-vinda's era and Terence McKenna in recent years have argued:

> The main medium of this so-called consciousness-expansion is LSD, and its prophets who propagate it as a substitute for meditation are characteristically only those who have neither experience nor qualification in the field of meditation. They have never gone through any serious spiritual training or sadhana, based on millennia of experience and psychological exploration, as handed down and taught by many of the great spiritual traditions of humanity.

In his treatise "Meditation," which was later expanded into the book *Creative Meditation and Multi-Dimnensional Consciousness*, Govinda once again is at work bridging the chasm between East and West, drawing the reader forward into a deeper, broader realm of experience, truly global, truly holistic:

> The East discovered the eternal recurrence of the same condi-tions and similar events. The West discovered the value of the uniqueness of each event or existential condition. The East kept its gaze fixed upon the cosmic background, the West on the indi-vidual foreground. The complete picture, however, combines foreground and background, integrating them into a higher unity. The complete human being, the person who has become whole (and therefore "holy"), unites the universal with the indi-vidual, the uniqueness of the moment with the eternity of the cyclic recurrence of constellations and existential situations.
>
> In the knowledge of immortality the East neglected the mundane life. In the knowledge of the uniqueness and value of the present moment, the West neglected the immortal. Only in the deepest aspects of the Vajrayāna (the mystic school of

Tibetan Buddhism), as well as in the I Ching (the oldest book of Chinese wisdom), has the attempt been made to connect the vision of the foreground with that of the background, to connect the momentary with the eternal and the uniqueness of every situation with the ever-recurring constellations of universal forces.

Like his treatise "Meditation," Govinda's essay "A New Way to Look at the I Ching" would later evolve into a book, *The Inner Structure of the I CHING*. In his study of the I Ching, Lama Govinda was looking for the key to unlock the ancient mysteries deeper than fortune-telling; he sought to articulate its deeper purpose, one beyond its popular use as a form of divination. For him, it was a work of great practical wisdom, which illuminated immutable laws and primordial elements, and he wanted to make it accessible again:

> The book may appear to most readers as a book of prophecies or oracles, as dark and mysterious as those of the Pythia of Delphi. But before it was converted into a mere oracle book, it had a clear system and structure that expressed a profound worldview. And this worldview is what interests us, irrespective of the fact that the I Ching might reveal the possibilities of our future. I say "possibilities," because this book was not written with the intention of revealing our fate or denying our free will, but rather to help us decide our way from the present into the future on the basis of generally prevailing laws. These laws are not meant to determine the future, but are indications stable enough to direct our course of action.
>
> If we know that fire burns, we shall avoid putting our hands into it. Nevertheless, the same fire that can hurt us, can serve us in many ways if we understand its nature and respect it. So

it is with all phenomena of the world; the more we respect and understand them, the easier will be the conditions of our life.

In "Questions and Answers, Human Dimensions Seminar, June 1975," Govinda patiently and generously responds to a number of questions on a variety of real-world concerns of spiritual seekers, including:

I would like to ask about mantras. I would like to know if there will ever be any American mantras, or if chanting must always be done in Sanskrit or in the Japanese language?

Would you please discuss attachment?

Should we meditate upon universal love?

What do you mean by concentration?

What do you mean by "cosmic play"?

What is the singing we sometimes hear in our ears when we are in meditation in a group?

His insightful answers to the aspirants who attended this seminar are as valid today as they were over a quarter of a century ago.

The Way of the White Cloud Leads to the Here and Now

Turning the pages of *The Lost Teachings*, a mood of joy and hopefulness arises; and it is borne to the surface of consciousness on a profound respect and gratitude for the legacy of Lama Govinda and Li Gotami.

Revisiting the vision of Teilhard de Chardin through the eyes of a great Tibetan Buddhist scholar and world citizen like Govinda is healing and inspiring. The work of Teilhard de Chardin takes on a new meaning, both poignant and urgent, in this era in which creationism and evolution are set against each other and religious fundamentalism has come to be seen in politics and the mass media as the face of Christianity. After all, Teilhard was both a philosopher and a paleontologist: he was present at the discovery of the Peking Man, and his masterpiece, *The Phenomenon of Man*, treats the book of Genesis not as literal narrative but as mystical metaphor.

Govinda's articulate and insightful arguments concerning the use of drugs as "mind-expanding" agents also have new meaning and a renewed relevancy. When Govinda first spoke out on this vital and controversial issue, Timothy Leary, the self-proclaimed "High Priest" of psychedelics, was a counterculture icon. But Leary's long strange trip ended badly. The arc of his saga stretched from teaching and doing research at Harvard University through participating in the "Human Be-Ins" of the late 1960s ("tune in, turn on, drop out"), being smuggled out of the United States and into exile in Algeria by the Weather Underground and the Black Panther Party, spending a stint in Soledad Prison in the cell next to Charles Manson, doing a lecture tour with Nixon White House aide and fellow felon G. Gordon Liddy, and videotaping his own death from prostate cancer. With the advent of techno-paganism, raves, smart drugs, Ecstasy, and the Burning Man phenomena in the 1990s and early 2000s, the issue of use of psychedelics for mind-expansion has returned and been recast.

Terence McKenna, a writer and philosopher, who died in 2000, was the successor to Leary (much less flamboyant, much less erratic, and therefore much more credible) in championing the hallucinogen experience. According to McKenna's "Stoned Ape" theory of human evolution, consuming mushrooms that grew in the dung of hoofed animals started the human species on its evolutionary spiral. McKenna postulated that the psilocybin content of those mushrooms led to the development of language and other powers; he also suggested that the decline of such properties in human diet has led over the last 12,000 years to a relapse into more savage, prehuman behavior.

Injecting Govinda's reasoned and authoritative view of so-called mind expansion from the ground of 2500 years of Buddhist psychology into the revived dialogue on these issues can only help elevate the discourse.

And in the light of current scientific research into the nature of the mind, it is also both heartening and illuminating to read anew Govinda's treatise on meditation. Consider the work of the Mind & Life Institute in Boulder, Colorado, where "studies on numerous meditators have shown that the practice can reshape the brain to react, for example, in more positive, open ways when confronted with challenges."[48] Matthieu Ricard, a French monk living at the Shechen Tennyi Dargyeling Monastery in Nepal, is one of the leadings participants in the Mind & Life Institute's research. And, indeed, of all of the luminaries on the contemporary scene, it is Ricard who personifies continuity with Govinda's example of serious scholarship fused with deeply personal, experiential commitment and a cross-cultural perspective.

After completing a doctoral thesis on molecular genetics at the Institut Pasteur, Ricard, son of esteemed French philosopher Jean-François Revel, chose to forsake the path of science and follow his karma to the Himalayas, where he became an intimate student and invaluable aide to the great Nyingmapa sage, Dilgo Khyentse Rinpoche, who was the Dalai Lama's Dzogchen meditation teacher. Like Govinda, Ricard has been a prodigious contributor to both the preservation and advancement of Tibetan Buddhism and the global dialogue on the interpenetrating problems and promises of spirituality and science. His eclectic body of works includes *Happiness: A Guide to Developing Life's Most Important Skill*, *The Quantum and The Lotus: A Journey to the Frontiers where Science and Buddhism Meet* (coauthored with Vietnamese astrophysicist Trinh

Xuan Thuan), and a translation of *The Life of Shabkar* (one of Tibet's great yogis of earlier ages).

The result of Ricard's work with the Institute of Mind & Life is compelling:

> Mr Ricard, who is the French interpreter for Tibet's spiritual leader, the Dalai Lama, took part in trials to show that brain training in the form of meditation can cause an overwhelming change in levels of happiness.
>
> MRI scans showed that he and other long-term meditators—who had completed more than 10,000 hours each—experienced a huge level of "positive emotions" in the left pre-frontal cortex of the brain, which is associated with happiness. The right-hand side, which handles negative thoughts, is suppressed.
>
> Further studies have shown that even novices who have done only a little meditation have increased levels of happiness. But Mr Ricard's abilities were head and shoulders above the others involved in the trials.
>
> "The mind is malleable," Mr Ricard told *The Independent* . . . . "Our life can be greatly transformed by even a minimal change in how we manage our thoughts and perceive and interpret the world. Happiness is a skill. It requires effort and time."[49]

The seeds of such research are planted in Govinda's writings on meditation from the 1960s and 1970s. Indeed, if he were alive today Govinda would probably be intimately involved in this or similar studies. At the very least, he would be following developments closely and holding forth for his visitors on the implications of what has been learned so far and on what direction the inquiry should take and what these pioneers should expect to encounter along the way, just as he did for Huston Smith, John Blofeld, Ken

Winkler, and the many others whose lives were touched by him and his beautiful wife, Li.

But, like many awakened mystical personalities, Lama Govinda and Li Gotami left behind something more than the words on the pages of this and other worthy tomes, something ineffable, yet seemingly palpable, something indescribable, and yet informative; this mysterious something is mirrored in their photo album. Almost invariably (the exceptions being from early in his life), photos of Lama Anagarika Govinda show him in the company of Li Gotami; and in these photos, without exception, the couple is clothed in the religious robes of their own design.

Govinda and Gotami were both accomplished painters, and Gotami was an accomplished photographer as well. Their shared sense of visual aesthetics served them well. Whether conscious, or simply second nature, their image itself conveys great meaning, and so much more than words, for example, the essential balance and vital interplay between yin and yang, yab and yum, male and female, consciousness and form, earth and sky, and all of it wrapped in sacredness. It is as if the couple emerged from some Nicholas Roerich painting to walk among us, communicating something by their very presence. And, indeed, in the religious art of Tibet it is common that Buddhas, Bodhisattvas, deities, and demigods are portrayed in connubial bliss with their consorts.

What is this ineffable, indescribable something? Nothing more or less than our own humanness: relatedness, touch, empathy, compassion, altruism, and the divinity it expresses.

From Theravada to Zen

To understand the sacred scriptures of Buddhism, we must be familiar to some extent with the living stream of tradition, as it has come down to us in unbroken continuity from the days of the Buddha. In spite of many differences in conception and formulation, even the comparatively later texts of the Mahayana are built upon the teachings of the earliest known tradition, which were already subdivided into eighteen different schools, each having its own canonical scriptures. However, only one of these canons has survived intact up to the present day, that of the Theravadins, the teachings of the Elders. The reason for their survival was their insular seclusion in Ceylon, due to which they remained untouched by the spiritual and political revolutions on the mainland of India and the rest of Asia.

Until now the West has been mainly familiarized with the texts of this school, so that many people have formed the conviction that Theravada is the only authentic form of Buddhism, as taught by the Buddha. We must remember, however, that not less than four centuries had passed before the Pali canon was put down in writing. Even if we want to trust the Indian capacity to pass on faithfully the words of the great religious leaders orally from Guru to Chela for centuries on end, we must not forget that words are not lifeless objects, but that they possess many meanings and associations of a spiritual and emotional nature, so that people of different temperaments, different backgrounds, and different mentalities—to say nothing of people belonging to different centuries—will associate different meanings, or only a certain aspect of the original meaning, with the same words.

This divergence is made evident in the fact that by the time the Theravada canon had been fixed, eighteen different Buddhist schools had already come into existence. No conscientious and unprejudiced scholar can overlook this fact, and therefore we must give to each of the different traditions as much credence as we are willing to give to the Theravadins. Each has an equal claim of representing a true aspect of the teachings of the Buddha and a sincere effort to preserve as much as possible of the original words and thoughts of the Enlightened One. Only in this way can we obtain a complete and genuine picture of Buddhist thought and experience that reveals the whole wealth of Buddhist culture and its application in life, a picture that not only enriches our knowledge, but also deepens the meaning and the importance of every single phase or school of Buddhism. Such knowledge is equally essential for understanding the Pali scriptures of the Theravadins, as it is for understanding the other contemporary Hinayana schools and the Mahayana, which finally took over the mainstream of Buddhist traditions and carried it all over Southeast Asia, into the Far East, and into Central Asia.

Only a detailed study of the Dharma theory in the scriptures of the Sarvāstivādins and of the Mahayana made it possible to see the teachings of the Theravadins in their true perspective and to arrive at a deeper understanding of their philosophical and metaphysical foundations. The one-sided opinion of earlier scholars was that

Buddhism is a system without any metaphysical background, floating in a kind of spiritual vacuum. This view represented the teachings of the Buddha as a cold intellectual doctrine that fitted more into the European Age of Reason (which coincided with the beginnings of Buddhist research) than with the religion that inspired one third of humanity with hope and faith.

Helmuth von Glasenapp, well known for his impartial works on the history of Buddhist thought, says, "The fact that formerly nothing was known about the Dharma theory, is the cause that many scholars missed a metaphysical foundation in the canonical discourse, and therefore declared the Buddha—according to their respective temperament—as an agnostic or a mere teacher of ethics, or they deduced from his silence about God, soul, and other concepts which contradict the Dharma theory, a mystic secret doctrine about Atman, etc." Glasenapp is even more outspoken in another article, in which he explains the Buddhist concept of *dhammas* (the Pali version of the Sanskrit *dharmas*) whose cooperation, according to their inherent law, brings about what we conceive of as "personality" and the "world" experienced by it.

> This is a concept whose fundamental importance for the Buddhist view of the world and its doctrine of salvation has been revealed only in the course of the last thirty years. Since the word *"dhamma"* (literally, the supporting element) has already in Pali several meanings (universal law, righteousness, duty, property, object), one did not realize that besides these many meanings, it is used in the Pali Canon also as a terminus technicus for the ultimate, irreducible factors out of which everything is composed that we believe to perceive within and without ourselves. Since this fundamental concept of Buddhist philosophy had not been understood in its true significance, one could only appreciate the Buddha's ethical principles and his doctrine of liberation;

however, one could not realize that the practical side has a theoretical foundation, a "philosophy of becoming," which is unique in the spiritual history of humanity, in so far as it explains everything that exists through the co-operation of only momentary existing forces arising and disappearing in functional dependence on each other. Due to this, Buddhism can renounce the concept of eternal substances (matter, soul, God) which in all other teachings form the supporting basis.

Here we come to the core of the problem. What distinguished the Buddha from his contemporaries, and what raised him above the general spiritual attitude of his country, was his perception of the dynamic nature of reality. The Four Noble Truths (the truth of suffering, its origin, its annihilation, and the way leading to its annihilation) as well as the Eightfold Path toward liberation form the general Indian frame of his teachings, but not what gives Buddhism its specific character. But when the Buddha put the *anātman* idea into the center of his teaching, he took the decisive step from a static to a dynamic view of the world, from an emphasis on "being" to an emphasis on "becoming," from the concept of an unchangeable permanent "I" (ego) to the realization of the interdependence of all forms and aspects of life and the capacity of individuals to grow beyond themselves and their self-created limitations. Thus the insurmountable contrast between "I" and world, mind and matter, substance and appearance, the eternal and the impermanent, etc., was eliminated.

The doctrine of the Buddha is the antithesis of the concept of "substance" that has governed human thought for millennia. Just as Einstein's theory of relativity influenced and changed the entire body of modern thinking, in a similar way the anātman idea of the Buddha caused a revolution in Indian thought. This revolution did not imply a negation of the religious principles of the past or a skeptical attitude toward metaphysical values; it was more in the nature of a revaluation of these ideas in the light of experience and of a new spiritual perspective. The Buddha never doubted the continuity of life beyond death, nor the existence and attainability of higher states of existence and their influence on human life. He did not doubt the existence of a moral law, nor that of a universe governed by equally strict and unalterable laws, and the world in which he lived was for him not merely a material phenomenon, but a manifestation of living and conscious forces. It was a world thoroughly alive with psychic forces in a way unimaginable to people of our times, as becomes all too apparent in the soulless and equally uninspiring interpretation of Buddhism by modern Buddhists, who confound the anātman idea with "soullessness," a term conveying a totally wrong impression. How can we speak about Buddhist psychology without presupposing a psyche? The Buddha rejected the idea of an eternal, unchangeable soul substance, existing as a separate entity or monad, but he never denied the existence of consciously directed spiritual and psychic forces, which in spite of their constant flow and change of form and appearance retained their continuity and organic unity. The human being is not a mere mechanism of elements that have been thrown together by blind chance, but a conscious organism following its own inherent rules in which individual tendencies and universal laws are in constant cooperation.

The Buddha freed the world of its "thingishness" as well as of its mere "illusionness" by opposing a dogmatically hardened and misunderstood ātmavāda—which originally was born from an experience of inner reality, the living breath of the universe within us, but which in the course of time had frozen into the concept of an unchangeable individual self. The Buddha replaced the idea of an immutable, eternal soul monad incapable of growth and development with the conception of a spiritual consciousness yearning

5

for freedom and highest enlightenment, and capable of attaining this supreme goal in the course of a continuous process of becoming and dissolving.

In this process of transformation, we find not only the source of transience and suffering, but also the source of all spiritual life and growth. When the Buddha spoke about this suffering, it was not an outcome of pessimism or world-weariness, but due to the realization that unless we recognize the nature and cause of our suffering, we cannot make use of the tremendous potentialities of our mind and attain a state of perfect enlightenment, which will reveal the universality of our innermost being. In this context, "suffering" is only another word for our imperfection and our wrong attitude. This realization was not founded on logical conclusions, but on the Buddha's own experience in attaining illumination, in which he transcended the limitations of individuality by overcoming the illusion of egohood. Overcoming this illusion does not mean that his individuality was annihilated, but only that he no longer mistook it as the essence of his being, seeing it instead as only a vehicle, a necessary means to become conscious of his universality, the universality of the all-embracing mind.

Looking back from this experience of highest reality and self-realization, the Enlightened One saw the world in a reversed perspective (reversed from the point of view of the ordinary person), namely in the perspective of the anātman idea; and lo, this apparently inescapable, solid and substantial world, dissolved into a whirling nebulous mass of insubstantial, eternally rotating elements of continually arising and disintegrating forms. The momentariness of these elements of existence (dharmas), which make up the river of life and of all phenomena, makes it impossible to apply concepts like "being" and "non-being" to them.

The world, O Kaccāna, is given to dualism, to the "it is" and the "it is not." He, however, O Kaccāna, who has realized with perfect wisdom how things arise in this world, for him, there is no "it is not" in this world. And he, O Kaccāna, who realizes with perfect wisdom how things disappear in this world, for him, there is no "it is" in the world.[1]

Being and non-being can only be applied to things or substances existing "in themselves," that is, to absolute units, as represented by our abstract concepts; they can never be applied to anything real or actual, because no thing and no being can exist in itself or for itself, but only in relationship to other things or beings, to conscious or unconscious forces in the universe. Concepts like "identity" and "non-identity" therefore lose their meaning. For this reason, the Sage Nagasena answered King Milinda's question about whether the doer is identical with the reaper of the fruit of the action (whether in this or in a following life), "Na ca so, na ca añño." "He is neither the same, nor a different one."[2]

The Buddha, therefore, replaces the concepts of identity and non-identity (which both represent extremes of abstract thought) by the formula of dependent origination (*pratītya-samutpāda*). This was much more than the proclamation of a scientific law of causation, as superficial observers maintained in order to prove the similarity to their own soulless and mechanistic worldview. Their causality presupposes a purely time-conditioned, unalterable sequence of events, that is, a necessary and predictable course of action.

The pratītya-samutpāda, however, is not confined to a sequence in time, but can also be interpreted as a simultaneous cooperation of all its links, insofar as each of them represents the sum total of all the others, seen under a particular aspect. In other words, from the point of view of time and of the course of individual existence, that is, from the mundane point of view, the formula of dependent origination can be interpreted causally, but not, however, from the standpoint of the highest truth (*paramārtha*).

To a certain extent, the causal interpretation is a concession toward a more popular understanding, one that requires a concrete example related to actual life and not a strictly logical, scientific formula. Therefore, we find even in the Pali texts no uniformity in the presentation of this formula, in which sometimes several links are left out and even the reversibility of the sequence of certain links has been pointed out. This is not due to lack of logical thinking as some critics assumed, but shows that the originators of these different formulations wanted to demonstrate that they were not concerned with a strictly time-conditioned sequence of phenomena in which one would follow another with mechanical necessity. What they wanted to point out was the non-substantiality and relativity of all individual phenomena, none of which exists in its own nature, independent of all other factors of life. Therefore, they are described as *śūnyam*: empty of self-nature, non-absolute.

Since no first beginning of any individual or of any inner or outer phenomena can be found, each has the totality of the universe as its base. Or, to express this concept from the standpoint of time, we could say that each of these phenomena, and especially every individual, has an infinite past and is therefore based on an infinity of relations, which do not and cannot exclude anything that ever existed or is liable to come into existence. Therefore, all individuals (or rather all who have an individual existence) have the whole universe as their common ground, and this universality becomes conscious in the experience of enlightenment, in which the individual awakens to its true, all-embracing nature.

To become conscious of this all-embracing nature, we have to empty ourselves of all conceptual thought and discriminating perception. This emptiness (śūnyatā) is not a negative property, but a state of freedom from impediments and limitations, a state of spontaneous receptivity in which we open up to the all-inclusive reality of a higher dimension. Here we realize the śūnyatā that forms the central concept of the Prajnaparamita Sutra. Far from being the expression of a nihilistic philosophy, which denies all reality, it is the logical consequence of the anātman doctrine of non-substantiality. Śūnyatā is the emptiness of all conceptual designations and at the same time the recognition of a higher, incommensurable, and indefinable reality, which can be experienced only in the state of perfect enlightenment.

While we are able to come to an understanding of relativity through reasoning, the experience of universality and completeness can be attained only when all conceptual thought (*kalpana*), all word-thinking has come to rest. Realization of the teachings of the Prajnaparamita Sutra can only come about on the path of meditative practice (*yogācāra*), through a transformation of our consciousness. Meditation in this sense is therefore not a search after intellectual solutions or an analysis of worldly phenomena with worldly means—which would merely be a moving around in circles—but a breaking out from this circle, an abandoning of our thought habits in order "to reach the other shore" (as has been said not only in the Prajnaparamita-hridaya, but already in the ancient Sutta-Nipāta[3]). A complete reversal or spiritual transformation is required, a "turning about in the deepest seat of our consciousness," as expressed in the Lankāvatāra Sutra.[4] This reversal brings about a new spiritual outlook, similar to what the Buddha experienced when returning from the Tree of Enlightenment. A new dimension of consciousness is being opened by this experience. This dimension transcends the limits of mundane thought.

The exploration of this consciousness, which goes beyond the boundaries of individual existence, is the special merit of the Vijñānavādins (or Yogācārins, as they were also called) because they were not content merely with a theoretical exploration, and regarded practical experience as the only legitimate way to acquire true knowledge. For them, consciousness itself, not the thought process, is the ultimate judge of reality; and the deeper we descend into this reality, the clearer will its true nature reveal itself—a nature before which all words turn back, because only negations like "infinity," "timelessness," "emptiness," and the like can hint at the enormity of the experience. In the universality of this primordial ground of consciousness, the Vijñānavādins discovered the source of all forms of existence, their dependent origination and transformation, and also their coming to rest in the state of perfect enlightenment.

If we give credence to the early scriptures of Buddhism, which without exception agree in their description of the Buddha's enlightenment, we can have no doubt that here we are confronted with an experience of such all-embracing universality that all limitations of time and space were transcended, and with them the illusions of the substantiality of our empirical world and of our separate egohood.

Recognizing this experience as the real starting point of Buddhism and not as only a distant, more or less theoretical aim or ideal, the followers of Ch'an Buddhism in China and of Zen in Japan try to go back to the very origin of Buddhist tradition by insisting on the spontaneity of the human mind, which basically is not different from that of the Buddha, if only we can free it from the cobwebs of habitual thought and prejudice. They maintain that we have to replace book knowledge by direct experience, scholarliness by intuition, and the historical Buddha by the Buddha within us—by awakening the potentialities of our mind, which will lead to the realization of perfect enlightenment. It is a courageous attempt that requires complete self-dedication and complete surrender of one's whole being, without reservations, without holding back anything to which our ego can cling. It is like playing *va banque* on the spiritual plane, a game in which one may gain everything or lose everything—because to miss the aim even by a hair's breadth is equal to being worlds apart from it. The Ch'an practice has therefore been compared to a leap into a bottomless abyss, a letting go of all familiar ideas and prejudices. The abyss is the unfathomable depth of our own consciousness, which yawns beyond the narrow circle of our egocentric world of illusions. In order to find the courage to leap into the depth, we require a certain inner preparation and a spiritual stimulus that is strong enough to take the risk. Unless the mind has become mature enough to recognize or to become aware of its own depth, there will be no urge to explore it and no faith in the final result of this daring undertaking. Here is where the faith in the Buddha, as one who has gone this way (which is the meaning of the appellation "Tathagata"), comes in, a faith justified by the result and the example of his life and the lasting effect it had on all who followed him. But unless we are ready to take the risks the Buddha took when he set out on his lonely way to enlightenment in the forest of Uruvela, nothing can be gained. Those who feel content in their ignorance or in their limited knowledge will have no inclination to take this risk, either because they have not yet reached the point where the problem begins or because they trust the flimsy superstructure of their logical speculations under which the problem has been buried. The former know nothing of the gaping abyss; the latter believe they can bridge it intellectually.

The followers of Ch'an and Zen, however, know that all logical and philosophical solutions and definitions are limited and one-sided, because reality lies beyond all contradictory, mutually exclusive pairs of opposites with which our two-dimensional logic deals. They therefore use their thought activity only as a means to become conscious of the unthinkable and to realize the problematic character of the world and the mystery of their own existence, without expecting solutions that go beyond the limited nature of their intellect. They therefore try to avoid ready-made mental associations and judgments, and endeavor to remain in a state of pure contemplation, seeing things as if they were seeing them for the first time—spontaneously, without prejudice, free from likes and dislikes.

In this way, everything will become a wonder and a door to the great mystery of life, behind which the wealth of the whole universe is hidden, together with the Great Emptiness that makes plentitude possible, though it may frighten us, because it is so inconceivable to our senses and appears so abysmal to our ego-centered consciousness (bent as it is to maintain its own identity). If we could give up this egocentric, discriminating, and dissecting attitude of the intellect even for one moment, the true nature of all things would manifest themselves "like the sun that rises through empty space and illuminates the whole universe unhindered and without limits." In other words, as soon as we succeed in silencing the restless activity of our intellect and give our intuition a chance, the pure all-embracing spirit in us will manifest itself. We don't need to shun sense activities, or the perception of sense objects, but only our ego-conditioned judgments and attitudes. We must understand that the true spirit, the depth consciousness, expresses itself in these perceptions and sense activities, without being dependent on them. We should not form judgments on the ground of such perceptions, nor should we allow our thoughts to be determined and led by them. And yet we should abstain from renouncing them in the pursuance of religious aims or from imagining the universal consciousness as something separate from us. (For this reason the Buddha rejected asceticism and replaced it by control of, but not suppression of the senses.) We should neither cling to the senses, nor renounce them, but we should remain independent of everything that is either above or below us or around us. There is no place where Ch'an (*dhyāna*, the way of inner vision) could not be practiced, because it is concerned not with an ascetic negation of the senses or the material world as conceived by the senses, but with the gaining of a deeper, wider, more universal consciousness. Such a consciousness comprises both sides of reality: finite and infinite, material and immaterial, mind and matter, form and formless, impermanent and eternal, conditioned and unconditioned.

The more and longer we abstain from seeing things habitually, the more we shall realize their inconceivable, essentially unlimited nature. Habit kills intuition, because habit prevents living experience, direct perception. When our thinking has advanced to the point where the existential problem arises, we should not allow ourselves to be satisfied with intellectual solutions or lose ourselves in the pursuance of facts, figures, proofs, and abstract truths, which although incontrovertible have no bearing on life, or which (as in the case of science) create more problems than they can solve. Instead, we should have the courage to penetrate to the very limits of thought, where words become paradoxes and logic turns against itself.

The moment we open our inner eye instead of looking outward into a world of apparent material reality, illusion disappears, and we suddenly become aware of true reality. This is why the Dhyāna school speaks of "sudden enlightenment." It is a reversal of our perspective, a new orientation that leads to a revaluation of all values. Due to this opening of the inner eye, the world of sense perception loses its absoluteness and substantiality, and takes its rightful place in the order of relative and time-conditioned phenomena. Here begins the path of the Buddha—the path toward the realization of Buddhahood within ourselves—as represented by the main meditation schools of Mahayana Buddhism like Ch'an and Zen.

Meditation was always the main requisite of the Buddhist doctrine of liberation. However, the more the different techniques of meditation, their psychological definitions, and their metaphysical and philosophical principles were explained, classified, and fixed in commentaries and sub-commentaries, the more the practice of meditation was neglected and suffocated by theoretical discussions, moral rules and regulations, and endless recitations of sacred texts. The reaction was a revolt against scriptures and learnedness and a return to a more spontaneous and direct experience. The pedantry of scholastic thought and intellectual logic was countered by the weapon of the paradox, which like a sharp sword, cut through the knots of artificially created problems with the speed of a lightning flash, offering a glimpse of the true nature of things. The paradox, however, is a double-edged sword. As soon as it becomes a matter of routine, it destroys the very thing it helped to reveal. The force of the paradox, like that of a sword, lies in the unexpectedness and speed with which it is handled—otherwise it is no better than the knife in the hand of a butcher.

As an example for the ideal use of paradoxes, we may mention the Sutra of the Sixth Patriarch. He succeeded in expressing the spiritual attitude of Ch'an in a way that neither offends our common sense nor attempts to make common sense the measure of all things. Readers of this scripture are introduced from the very beginning into the right atmosphere, which enables them to rise from the plane of their everyday consciousness to the spontaneous participation in the reality of the higher level of consciousness. The figure of the Sixth Patriarch impresses us by his natural spontaneity, which should be inherent in every human being and with which the unprejudiced reader can easily identify. In this way, we are able to participate inwardly in the experiences and teachings of the Sixth Patriarch, whose very life has become a symbol of Ch'an Buddhism at its best.

The novice of Kwang-tung, whose mind was not yet burdened by any philosophical problem, penetrates spontaneously into the center of spiritual life: the experience of Buddhahood. This experience does not depend on monastic rules and learnedness, on asceticism and virtuousness, on book knowledge and recitation of sacred texts, but only on the realization of the living spirit within us.

The Sixth Patriarch attained to a state of spontaneous enlightenment without study and book knowledge, though on the other hand it was through listening to the recitation of the Diamond Sutra that his interest was aroused and his spiritual eye was opened. Spontaneous experience, therefore, can very well be the product of an ancient hallowed tradition, if this tradition contains symbols of a supramental reality of formulations that lead the mind beyond the narrow circle of mundane reasoning. In the unexpected clash between a sensitive mind and such symbols and formulations, the doors of inner perception are suddenly opened, enabling the individual to identify with the supramental reality contained in those mysterious formulations and symbols.

The Sixth Patriarch came from a good but impoverished family in Kwang-tung. One day while he was selling firewood in the market of Canton, he listened to the recitation of the Diamond Sutra, and it evoked such a deep response in him that he decided to enter a monastery of the Ch'an school, whose abbot was the Fifth Patriarch. He became a novice there and as such was given the lowliest work in the monastery's stable and kitchen. One day the abbot called together all his disciples in order to choose his successor. He asked them to write a stanza about the innermost nature of the mind. However, nobody dared to do so, with the exception of the learned Shin-shau, whom everybody already regarded as the successor of the Fifth Patriarch. He wrote his verse on the wall of the corridor, in order to find out the opinion of the Patriarch and to announce his authorship only if the Patriarch was pleased with the stanza. However, though the Patriarch praised the lines, he asked Shin-shau to meditate upon them a few days more and then to write another stanza showing that its author had passed through "the gates of enlightenment," in other words, that he had really experienced what he wrote about.

Two days later it happened that a young man who passed by the room in which the young novice from Kwang-tung was husking rice recited aloud the stanza of Shin-shau. The novice thereupon went into the corridor where Shin-shau had written his stanza and asked a visitor he met there by chance to read the verse for him, since he himself could neither read nor write. After the visitor had read out the verse to him, the novice said that he had also composed a stanza and asked the visitor to write it under the lines of Shin-shau.

When the other monks saw the new stanza, they were filled with wonder and said, "How was it possible that we allowed such an enlightened person to work for us?" But the Patriarch feared that the jealousy of the other monks might lead them to harm the novice if they knew he was to become the successor, so he erased the stanza with one of his sandals and asked the young man to call on him during the night. When everybody in the monastery was deep asleep, he gave the novice the insignias of his future office and made him the Sixth Patriarch. The Fifth Patriarch then bade him to leave the monastery at once and return only after his predecessor had passed away. The novice did so, and when he returned with the robes of office, he was recognized as the Sixth Patriarch.

Let us now consider the stanzas of Shin-shau and of the Sixth Patriarch, because they give us a valuable insight into the mental attitude of the Ch'an school. The stanza of Shin-shau ran:

> Our body is like a bodhi-tree,
> Our mind is like a clear mirror;
> From hour to hour it must be cleansed,
> So that no dust can collect upon it.[5]

Apart from showing a pedantic concern for the preservation of the purity of the "inner mirror" (the Original Mind—which is at any rate beyond "purity" and "impurity"), this verse also shows that the author does not speak from his own experiences, but only as a man of letters, because the verse is based on a saying in the Svetasvatara Upanishad:

> As a metal disk (mirror), tarnished by dust, shines bright again
> after it has been cleaned, so is the one incarnate person satisfied
> and free from grief, after he has seen the real nature of self.[6]

Thus, Shin-shau was only repeating the standpoint of the Upanishads without having experienced the reality of the Original Mind, while the young novice, in grasping the quintessence of the Diamond Sutra in an act of direct perception, had experienced in that moment the true nature of the mind, as is shown by his stanza, which at the same time rejects that of Shin-shau by revealing the Buddhist point of view understood by the masters of Ch'an:

> The Bodhi is not a tree at all,
> Nor is the mind a case of mirrors.
> When everything is empty,
> Where could the dust collect?[7]

The Original Mind, realized as the "Buddha Mind" or the principle of *bodhi*, which is a latent property of every consciousness, is not only a reflection of the universe—something that "mirrors" the universe—but is the universal reality itself. To the limited intellect, it can only appear as a kind of metaphysical emptiness, the absence of all qualities and possibilities of definition. Therefore, bodhi is not something that has originated or grown like a tree, neither is the mind a mere mirror, which only reflects reality in a secondary capacity. Since the mind is itself the all-embracing emptiness (śūnyatā), where could the dust ever collect? "The essence of the mind is great, we say, because it embraces all things, for all things are of our nature." Thus it is not a question of improving or cleansing our mind, but of becoming conscious of its universality. What we can improve is our intellect, our limited individual consciousness. However, doing so can never lead us beyond its own limits, because we remain inside the strictly circumscribed circle of its inherent laws (of time and space, logic, causality, etc.). Only the leap across the boundary, the giving up of all the contents that fetter us to those laws, can give us the experience of the totality of the spirit and the realization of its true nature, which is what we call enlightenment.

The true nature of our mind embraces all that lives. The Bodhisattva vow to free all living beings is therefore not as presumptuous as it sounds. It is not born from the illusion that a mortal man could set himself up as the savior of all beings or the redeemer of the whole world; it is, indeed, an outcome of the realization that only in the state of enlightenment will we be able to become one with all that lives. In this act of unification, we liberate ourselves and all living beings that are potentially present and are part of it in the deepest sense. For this reason, according to the Mahayana teachings, the liberation from one's own sufferings, the mere extinction of the will to live and of all ·desires, is regarded as insufficient, and the striving after perfect enlightenment (samyak-sambodhi) is regarded as the only goal worthy of a follower of the Buddha. As long as we despise the world and merely try to escape from it, we have neither overcome it nor mastered it and are far from having attained liberation. Therefore, this world is said to be the Buddha-world, within which enlightenment can be found. To search after enlightenment by separating oneself from the world is as foolish as to search for the horn of a hare. For one who treads earnestly the path of the world will not see the faults of the world.

In a similar way, we should not imagine that we attain enlightenment by the suppression of thought or our intellectual faculties. "It is a great mistake to suppress all thought," says Wai-Lang, the Sixth Patriarch.[8] Ch'an is the way to overcome the limitations of our intellectual attitude. But before we are able to appreciate Ch'an, we first must have developed our intellect, our capacity to think, to reason, and to discern. We cannot overcome or go beyond the intellect, if we never had one, if we never developed and mastered it, because only what we master is truly our own. The intellect is as necessary for overcoming mere emotionality and muddleheadedness as intuition is necessary for overcoming the limitations of the intellect and its discriminations.

Reason, the highest property of the intellect, is what guides our purposive thought. Purposes, however, are limited; therefore, reason can only operate in what is limited. Wisdom (prajna) alone can accept and intuitively realize the unlimited, the timeless and infinite—by renouncing explanations and recognizing the mystery, which can only be felt, experienced, and finally realized in life (but which can never be defined). Wisdom has its roots in experience, in the realization of our innermost being. Reason has its roots in thought. Yet wisdom will not despise either thought or reason, but will use them where they belong, namely in the realm of purposeful action, as well as for science and for coordinating our sense impressions, perceptions, sensations, feelings, and emotions into a meaningful whole.

Here the creative side of our thought—which converts the raw material of experience into a reasonable world—comes into play. How big or how small this world is, depends on the creative faculty of the individual mind. The small mind lives in the world of its ephemeral needs and desires; the great mind lives in the infinity of the universe and in the constant awareness of that fathomless mystery. This fathomless mystery gives depth and width to life and thus prevents us from mistaking the sense world for ultimate reality. Those who have penetrated to the limits of thought dare to take the leap into the Great Emptiness, the primordial ground of their own boundless being.

The Act of Will and
Its Role in the
Practice of Meditation

The world is said to be in the grip of a "power crisis," but few people realize that this statement is true in a much deeper sense than that of a mere economic problem. Power has become a human obsession and a self-destructive principle. At the same time it has resulted in a psychological revolt against the very root of power, namely the human intellect and the human will, which have led to the domination and misuse of the forces of nature and may result in the gradual destruction of our planet's ecology and the human race.

The psychological revolt has taken two forms: that of trying to escape the intellect and responsible action, and that of overcoming the intellect and its desire-bound volitions by turning away from the external world and trying to take refuge in meditative practices—in which subconscious and unconscious forces are awakened without a clear understanding of their nature and without the capacity to integrate them.

Under the circumstances it is no wonder that the human will has come into disrepute and is identified with the concept of power, and especially ego power, that either disassociates the individual from the universe or acts as a repressive force of certain qualities of human nature. Due to this misconception, the importance of the human will has been consistently pushed into the background of popular modern psychology, so that more and more the impression has been created that the human being is merely a product of biological drives, urges, and compulsions determined and conditioned by forces and circumstances beyond the individual's control.

At such a time it is good to be reminded by Dr. Roberto Assagioli's book *The Act of Will* that in spite of all these subconscious drives and conditioned reflexes the role of the conscious will is of decisive importance not only in the intellectual life of individuals, but even more so in the fulfillment of their spiritual aspirations and creative faculties. It is the basis of our sense of self-responsibility and therefore of all ethical values, without which human existence is unthinkable. In fact, without it, human existence would become meaningless. It is the basis of all religious thought and experience.

Only the narrow conception of the will as "something stern and forbidding, which condemns and represses most of the other aspects of human nature"[1] has created the present misunderstanding about the nature and function of the will, because the will cannot be separated from the discriminative and directive functions of consciousness. By artificially separating these functions in our conceptual terminology, we create a nonexistent problem. No will arises without a discerning consciousness. Thus a differentiating and focalized consciousness is the precondition for generating the directive force of the will, which thus is not a biological force, like those unconscious and subconscious drives, but a psychological one.

To put it in Assagioli's words, "The will has a *directive* and *regulatory* function—it balances and constructively utilizes all the other activities and energies of the human being without repressing them." Assagioli compares the function of the will to the helmsman of a ship: "He knows what the ship's course should be, and he keeps her steadily on it, despite the drifts caused by wind and current. But the power he needs to turn the wheel is altogether different from that required to propel the ship through the water, whether it be generated by engines, pressure of the winds on the sail, or the efforts of the rowers."[2]

Here wind, currents, and other forces correspond to biological drives, environmental conditions, and universal forces by which the individual is *conditioned*, but not wholly or exclusively determined. Here is where the principle of "free will" comes in, namely in the form of *knowledge* that permits an alternative between a right and a wrong decision, or between a more favorable and a less favorable decision, or between two equally acceptable alternatives. Thus, the actions of the helmsman (the conscious individual) are prompted by *knowledge* of "what the ship's course should be," in accordance with the chosen destination.

In other words, the nature of our will depends on the level of our knowledge. So long as human beings conceive themselves as independent or separate "egos," their will is egocentrically determined and limited. The moment they conceive and experience the self in perfect relationship and harmony with their surroundings and fellow beings, their will takes on a transpersonal quality.

If individuals realize they are an exponent of the totality of the universe, their will becomes the expression of that universal law, which Indian philosophy calls "dharma" and which manifests itself in the human heart (or the innermost center) as the realization of the highest spirit or the universal consciousness. Here the power aspect, the will to dominate, to control, to suppress, or to resist, disappears and makes room for a state of profound harmony.

Thus a proper understanding of the will includes a clear and balanced view of its dual nature: two different but not contradictory poles. On the one hand, the "power element" needs to be recognized, appreciated, if necessary strengthened, and then wisely applied. At the same time, we must recognize that there are volitional acts that do not necessarily require effort.

For instance, in the more advanced stages of meditation and contemplation, inspirational and institutional powers take over from the conceptual and intentional motivations, which have their justification and their proper places in the initial stages of meditative practice. In these higher stages, the personal will is effortless because, according to Assagioli, "The willer is so identified with the Transpersonal Will, or, at a still higher and more inclusive level, with the Universal Will, that his activities are accomplished with free spontaneity, a state in which he feels himself to be a willing channel into and through which powerful energies flow and operate."[3]

The concept of "will" thus takes on different meanings on different levels of consciousness, and Assagioli therefore distinguishes the various aspects of the human will as the "Strong Will" (in which we recognize the will as a dynamic force), the "Skillful Will" (in which we recognize "the ability to obtain desired results with the least possible expenditure of energy"), the "Good Will" (in which skillful means are applied to altruistic purposes), the "Transpersonal Will" (which is the urge to find a meaning of life, the urge toward higher realization [Sanskrit: *Dharma chanda*]), and finally the "Universal Will" (in which the human will is in perfect harmony with the universal law [Dharma]).

These different aspects of the will on different levels solve one of the ever-recurring problems in the definition and practice of meditation. The one maintains that meditation employs willpower insofar as it is intentional, goal-directed, and concentrated; the other maintains that it is a state of complete freedom from thoughts, concepts, ideas, volitions, aims or goals, without discrimination, evaluation, or intellectual attitude—in fact, a state of pure awareness, of contemplation, of mere "being."

To illustrate this attitude, I may quote a few sentences of a recent essay, "Contemplation" by Alan Watts:

> You, considered as that ego, cannot get polar vision or cosmic consciousness. It might arise all of itself, as if by divine grace, but there is nothing, just nothing, you can do or not do to bring it about. . . .
>
> If this becomes clear, the effort to transform one's mind should collapse, and along with it the whole illusion that one is a separate center of consciousness to which experience happens and for which these happenings are problematic. This collapse would be then the state of contemplation, the realization that all is one.[4]

If we take the Buddha's advice (which has proved its value through the millennia and is equally valid for our time), namely to avoid extremes, both in thought and life, then we should recognize that to think ourselves different from the universe in which we live is one extreme, and to think ourselves identical with it is the other extreme. The real position is that we are neither the same nor different from the universe (just as, in a similar sense, we are neither the same nor different from the person we were yesterday or in our childhood), because we are not separate and unchangeable units or monads, but rather the product of infinite, interrelated causes and conditions, which in their totality correspond to the totality of the universe. The individual may be compared to a whirlpool in a moving stream: inseparable from it and yet not the same; of the same origin and yet different in form and appearance; creating a center by its own unique movement, and yet remaining part of the creative (universal) stream.

This view is beautifully expressed in the opening sentence of Watts's essay: "The individual is an aperture through which the whole energy of the universe is aware of self, a vortex of vibrations in which it realizes itself as man or beast, flower or star—not alone, but as central to all that surrounds it."[5]

How much nearer such symbolical and poetical language comes to reality than all merely logically constructed theories! Is not the hollow space (or emptiness) in the center of the vortex the very "aperture" through which the individual becomes capable of being the supreme vessel in which the universe becomes conscious of itself?

In this very notion lies the justification of individuality and the importance of the individual as the other pole of the universe, and as such, inseparable from it. The Vedantic standpoint of absolute oneness, which tries to ascribe reality only to the universal pole by denigrating the individual pole to a state of mere illusion, makes individual life meaningless, including all individual effort toward self-realization. Therefore, the contention that "all is One" does not eliminate the fact that oneness is meaningless without otherness, unity without diversity, and that diversity is born from an ever and infinitely progressing polarity.

Reality, therefore, does not reside in the abstract concept of undifferentiated oneness or sameness, but in the recognition of creative polarity, in which the tension between the positive and the negative pole creates the unifying spark of life and consciousness, in which alone oneness can be experienced. Thus, what we call "reality" would be better described as "actuality," because only what acts on us or through us can be experienced, and what cannot be experienced exists only as a concept.

Therefore, the standpoint of "all is One" is as one-sided as the standpoint "all is different": both are conceptual extremes, the one denying (or depreciating) the value of individuality and individual effort, the other denying the inherent universality of the individual, while overestimating the role of its willpower.

The first standpoint regards all techniques of meditational training as superfluous, if not absurd, and leaves the individual to the action of divine grace or the spontaneity of intuition; the second standpoint relies too much on force, routine-like training, and personal achievement and suppresses by its intentionality the spontaneous forces of intuitive insight.

Here, it seems to me, that the middle path (as proposed by the Buddha and advocated in Assagioli's attitude) is a sound method on the path of realization. It makes use of human endeavor and effort as well as intelligence (in form of clear thought and higher aspirations) as a starting point for meditation. The Buddha's illumination was, as Assagioli points out, "the result and the reward of his *willed* endeavor." And quoting D. T. Suzuki, "Enlightenment therefore must involve the *will as well as the intellect.* It is an act of intuition born of the will."

It is clear that this "will" is not the ego-motivated will of the ordinary self-seeking individual, but what Assagioli would term the "Transpersonal Will," a will that has been sublimated and transformed into a force, directed beyond all narrow aims and purposes, transcending individual limitations, and finally turning the individual into "a willing channel through which the powerful energies of the universe flow and operate."

As long as the individual bars this channel by its ego-directed will, its illusion of separateness, or by simply being unaware of this potential source of energies, it cannot make use of it. Meditational practices have, therefore, no other purpose than to awaken, to develop, and to strengthen the awareness of the individual, to remove the hindrances that stand in the way of the free flow of creative and life-giving energies, to open the mind to the infinite possibilities of experience, and to make it an instrument capable of integrating those experiences in actual life.

Even the greatest genius—whether a musician, a poet, a painter or sculptor, a great philosopher, or a scientist—has to prepare and to master the organs of receptivity, the medium of the creative activity and the laws governing it. Thus, the employment of conscious will, effort, directedness, and concentration are not impediments to spontaneity and intuition, but act to prepare the ground for the reception and integration of intuitive experience and spontaneous insight into the nature of reality.

Meditative training, therefore, has no other purpose than to put us into an attitude of receptivity, to strengthen our sensibilities, to make us a "willing channel" for the forces of inspiration. Inspiration, however, dissipates itself in merely momentary feelings of elevation and freedom, or in mere emotionality, unless it has been integrated into our very being by the creative act of giving it form or expression, because no force can act unless it is formed and directed. Herein lies the power of art, of clear thought or profound vision or the realization of a new dimension of consciousness, which changes and directs our attitude toward life by giving it a deeper meaning.

Without the creative act of the Transpersonal Will, neither drug-induced visions (which are not an expansion of consciousness but a confused transmission of neurological messages) nor the auto-hypnotic trance states of misguided meditative practices, have any spiritual value, but are merely attempts to escape the realities of life.

Another attempt of such an escape is "by returning to a primitive state of consciousness, to be reabsorbed into the 'mother,' into a prenatal state, to lose oneself in the collective life. This is the way of regression. The other is the above-mentioned way of transcendence, of rising above ordinary consciousness. So we need to face courageously and willingly the requirements for transcending the limitations of personal consciousness without losing the center of individual awareness. This is possible because individuality and universality are not mutually exclusive."[6]

To unite them in the final realization of the human mind in the state of enlightenment is not only the aim of Assagioli's Psychosynthesis, but also of all creative meditation, which means an attitude of mind that does not try to evade but rather to solve the problems of life. Psychoanalysis is a valuable tool in the exploration of the human mind, but unless it is followed by a synthesis its therapeutic effect is of limited value.

For this reason Assagioli's Psychosynthesis is of special importance for our time, in which the analytical attitude of a dissecting and discriminating intellect may lead to a dissolution or depreciation of the creative effort unless we recognize again the role of the human will as a conscious force, dependent on the level of our knowledge and imagination, which alone can free us from the tyranny of blind desires and compulsions.

Knowledge and imagination are the two interdependent sides or poles of consciousness. Knowledge is based on experience that has been stored in memory, while imagination is the creative application of knowledge or the intuitive quality of consciousness, a quasi-playful attitude, whose inherent impetus gradually creates a direction (or directedness) from which all works of art and all great discoveries of the human mind are born.

That intuition and willpower are not mutually exclusive, or even spontaneity and a training of mental or technical faculties (necessary for the creative expression, formulation, and realization of intuitive insight), is demonstrated by the lives and works of great artists and thinkers, whose creations involved sustained effort, perseverance, and intense concentration. However, the creative principle and the source of strength is the power of imagination, which inspires and guides the genius of man. "Of all the distinctions between man and animal, the characteristic gift which makes us human is the power to work with symbolic images: the gift of imagination. The power that man has over nature and himself lies in his command of imaginary experience."7

This understanding is the very foundation of Tantric meditation, which is practiced in India and Tibet and has spread its influence over the greater part of Asia up to the Far East, stimulating the greatest works of art and a literature that the West has only now started to explore.

According to William James, "Every image has in itself a motor element," and Assagioli formulates this fundamental law in the following sentences: "Images or mental pictures and ideas tend to produce the physical conditions and external acts that correspond to them." And vice-versa: "Attitudes, movements, and actions tend to evoke corresponding images and ideas; these in turn evoke or intensify corresponding emotions and feelings." Furthermore, "Attention, interest, affirmations, and repetitions reinforce the ideas, images, and psychological formations in which they are centered."8

In these words, we have a competent description of the main elements of meditation and spiritual training, in which both will and intuition have their place and in which training is no contradiction to spontaneity. In fact, "The power of images can be said to constitute a necessary intermediary between the will and the other psychological functions," and though "the will possesses no *direct* power over the intuitive function, . . . the will can perform a most helpful *indirect* action; it can create and keep clear the channel of communication along which the intuitive impressions descend."9

Just as the imagination stirs the will toward the actualization and realization of the contents of imagination, in the same way the will is capable of calling up and directing powerful or significant images. This capability is what Assagioli uses as a therapeutic method, which he calls "guided imagination."

As mentioned before, this technique has been practiced and developed especially in Tibet, except there the guidance was not left to the choice or the judgment of the individual practitioner or the spiritual guide, but was based on the collective experience of innumerable generations of *sādhakas* (religious practitioners), a living tradition of more than a millennium.

The West has still to learn a great deal from this accumulated experience, but a psychological approach of the depth and wisdom of Assagioli's Psychosynthesis will go a long way toward opening an understanding and toward establishing the importance of the act of will, both in practical life and in the art of meditation.

Chapter 3

Teilhard de Chardin in the Mirror of Eastern Thought

Teilhard de Chardin is probably the first exponent of modern Europe who openly says what in the East has been regarded for millenniums as the highest truth, namely that all living beings, and especially all conscious life, are not only the product of infinite combinations, permutations, and transformations of blind forces or elements, but also a continuous unfoldment and increase of consciousness, in which differentiation and integration, individuality and universality complement each other. What the East produced out of its own experience in the form of mythical or purely spiritual symbols, in the form of similes or metaphysical intuitions, gained in Teilhard de Chardin the form of clear, logically consequent thought.

A formulation based on experience naturally needs a different means of expression from the severely limited language of pure science, which depends on the strict methodology of deduction and definition. This difference, however, does not mean there must be a contradiction between science and experience; it means only that we have to deal with two different *forms* of human experience.

What is it now that makes Teilhard de Chardin so important for our time, so universal, may I say, that every corner of humanity is concerned and willing to listen? First, because he was both a profoundly religious man and an eminent scientist who raised science to the level of metaphysical knowledge and made religion into a knowledge of humanity, that is, a knowledge of the unfoldment of human consciousness, which not only concerns the individual, but also moves and enlivens the universe and becomes conscious of itself. In the language of religion, this unfoldment is the awakening of the divine consciousness in human beings; in the language of science, it is the awakening of human consciousness to the awareness of the universe and to the realization of the human being's essential universality and completeness.

Teilhard de Chardin raises himself above both the dogmatisms of science and any particular religious tradition. For the Buddhist, the idea of an exclusively liberating religion or philosophy, or of an absolute science, is unacceptable (and that is a characteristic of most of the religions of India and the Far East). We believe not only that there are many ways toward the knowledge of reality, but also that in each period of the world, at each time and in each culture, the same truth must be found in a new expression and a different form. But because several forms can express the same truth, we must not conclude that arbitrary expressions of one culture or civilization or of one particular epoch are equal to that of another. Such a conclusion would lead to a fruitless and superficial syncretism, but not toward a deeper understanding, which can only be gained if we consider each form in the frame of its relationships, its associations, and in the context of its organic, historical, and traditional connections.

In such a way of looking at things, we shall discover a deeper parallelism and a more essential similarity of ideas than in external similarities. Therefore, we should not object to the differences of scientific and religious observations or formulations, or be put off because of seemingly mutually exclusive teachings of different confessions, but we should try to discover the underlying reasons and the organic connections from which they originated. In Teilhard de Chardin, the religious experience and the scientific knowledge were bridged by an immense cosmic conception, through an intuitive understanding of connections such as those the East had found by meditative insight and exploration of the human psyche.

I am thinking here less of the philosophy of the modern Indian thinker Sri Aurobindo Ghoshe (in whose writings one may believe to have found a similarity with the ideas of Teilhard de Chardin, which perhaps has more to do with the fact that Sri Aurobindo had been educated in England and was familiar with the modern idea of evolution) than I am of the purely Indian idea of an evolution, free from all Western influences. It was already contained, though in a mythical form, in the Jātakas, the stories of the previous lives of the Buddha, and in later Hinduism in the incarnations of Vishnu, in which the divine rises from the lower forms of animal life or half-animal beings up to the complete state of humanness, as expressed in the luminous figure of the Buddha. The Jātakas, for those not acquainted with them, are a collection of four hundred stories showing the rise toward enlightenment through all the realms of bodily incarnation, and expressing the idea of a spiritual evolution from the lowest to the highest forms of life.

The fundamental difference between Darwin's idea and that of the Indian view of life is that the directing force of consciousness upon an immanent aim of the highest possible perfection and universality (which in the language of religion is called the realization of the divine or the state of enlightenment) is already expressed in the lowliest forms of life, and is contained even in the universal laws or the behavior of so-called inorganic matter.

In a lecture by Peter Elliot, the problem arose about how one can speak of a new emergence, with life appearing for the first time in organic form, if the complete cosmos is already alive, including what we call matter, or the inorganic world. I think we have understood him rightly if we can say that the completely new is the emergence of a new *dimension* of life, the creation of consciousness as a forming, self-perpetuating, and individualizing force or potentiality. And just as consciousness, even in its most primitive form, represents a new dimension of life, so this consciousness proceeds in its unfoldment from one dimension to another, so that we can speak of several dimensions of consciousness.

For example, one could imagine that the simplest beings belong to the first dimension, in which only one direction is possible, so to say, only a kind of linear consciousness without width, with only one direction of development (which is therefore also causally determined). Furthermore, the more developed beings belong to the second dimension and have a kind of surface consciousness with many possibilities of direction and a correspondingly greater freedom. In the third dimension, as we know it, we have the human space consciousness. Finally, since we already feel now that our three-dimensional space consciousness is no longer adequate for the discoveries of our time, we are compelled to postulate a fourth dimension and cannot deny the possibility of many higher dimensions (expressed in mathematics as "n" dimensions). This multidimensionality and our directedness toward the fourth dimension is the subject of Jean Gebser's philosophy, which in this connection should be explained in more detail.

It appears as if always before a new dimension becomes completely conscious, a premonition occurs of something for which we have not yet a proper name. So we appear to be engaged with the problem of time, because we feel that we are confronted with a dimension for which we have a premonition, a certain feeling of its existence, but which we cannot define with the language at our disposal, a language strictly circumscribed by the dimension in which we live. (For more on this subject, refer to my essay "The Mystery of Time."[1])

It could also be that what we call "time" nowadays will be something quite different in a higher form of consciousness, namely a new kind of motion. The concept of *dimension* contains the idea of *extension* or of *motion* and *direction*. A movement in a certain exclusive direction would, therefore, correspond to the lowest dimension, while each new possibility of motion in a direction hitherto unknown would indicate a higher dimension.

If we speak of a "higher" dimension, however, we should not take this in the sense of a spiritual value, but in a strictly mathematical sense of a higher numerical order. According to our standpoint, we may attach a spiritual value to it or not, just as in art we may view perspective as either a form of progress, in the sense of something better, or a rather superficial type of realism that distorts the actual proportions in favor of an optical illusion. The so-called aperspective art, for instance, would maintain this standpoint, in view of the great works of art that were created, before the introduction of perspective in the Renaissance. But if we look impartially at these matters, we shall find both standpoints equally justified and therefore spiritually valid.

The discovery of perspective was the discovery of the relativity of all things, a relativity that did not deny the real values on which it was based. But if perspective were treated as the summun bonum of art, and not as a mere form of expression of a certain feeling of space, it becomes a limitation and hindrance of art expression, as Jean Gebser has effectively shown. We must guard against the prejudice of value judgments. Only then can we enjoy art in all its expressions, whether it is perspective or aperspective or transparent (in which a deeper relativity or mutual relationship is revealed).

Each new reality is in danger of being overemphasized by its first discoverers or their imitators, so we find an overemphasis on perspective at the beginning of the Renaissance, which for this reason enjoyed architectural constructions. The small artists lived in

symptoms, which they regarded as essentials; the great artists created art in spite of the symptoms, because their experience was
mightier than the fashion of their time.

A bewildered public nowadays accepts as art anything that is
aperspective and beyond its understanding, not having any clear
conception of the meaning of art or of any standards of technical
knowledge. So innumerable works of apparent mediocrity pass as
art and are even accepted by museums and galleries, as if any permanent values were attached to them. But just as a jumble of pic-
turesque words or well-sounding rhymes do not make a poem if it
is devoid of sense, so no amount of harmonious colors (or disso-
nances) make a picture, if the artist has nothing to say or no experience to express. After all, art is a form of communication, and if we
want to communicate something, we must express ourselves in a
language of forms or sounds that convey something to the onlooker
or the hearer. If, however, we only want to express our private fantasies or feelings without wishing to communicate or because they
do not touch a common human experience, why then do we exhibit
them and expect a resonance from the public?

But to come back to the problem of the multidimensionality of
our world or our experience of it, when we think about the fourth
dimension or have an uncertain feeling about it (in the strange
realization that time seems to be more than mere "clock time" and
that within the concept of time we already can discern a great
number of categories), then we can only say that time is a certain
form of movement. And since we have exhausted the possibilities
of movement in three-dimensional space, only one other form
of movement remains. Instead of movement in external space, or
from the center of our consciousness outward, there is movement
in the reverse direction, from outside toward the center. The
result is a dimension in which time becomes again space, namely
interior space.

In this inner space, not only are the things of the past kept, but the possibility also exists to raise the past into the present and to recognize, and guide, the seeds of the future. As in the outer space, we distinguish also the objects of the past as near or distant ones, and we move between surface and depth. However, the further we penetrate into the depth, the more comprehensive our view becomes, because we have the whole universe as our foundation: our center is the common basis of all things and of all worlds, in which life and consciousness have their roots.

Today, humanity tries, from a desperate feeling that we stand upon the threshold of something new and without knowing where it will lead us, to conquer space. I ask myself if we are searching in the wrong direction, if we are making a methodological mistake, because what we search for in reality is hidden in the inner space of our depth consciousness, in which all space really is contained. Is it not perhaps that we project outward our unrecognized wish, or a desire arising from inner necessity, to explore the immense possibilities of that inner space by projecting ourselves into an infinite outer space in which, naturally, we never arrive at an ultimate aim or find a center? We simply lose ourselves in infinity. Nothing real will ever be achieved in this way.

The moment will come, therefore, when humanity will take a new direction, and it seems to me that this moment will perhaps not be far off, because we will see the impossibility of conquering outer space and will be obliged to turn toward inner space, in which everything we searched for in the outer world already exists.

In the description of his process of enlightenment, the Buddha traces his aeon-long path of development back to the cosmic origination and dissolution—blooming and waning, in beauty and terror, in powerful evolutions and revolutions—that follow each other like systole and diastole, or like the divine breath of infinite life, which finds its crowning climax in that timeless moment of "convergence," cosmic integration, in which the rivers of all time merge in the ocean of an all-embracing present.

Based on just such an experience, the Buddha established his doctrine of "the Middle Way," which denies neither the value of individuality, self-responsibility, and the decision of free will, with its result-producing action, nor the potential universality of the human being and the solidarity of all life.

Easterners (and especially Indians), due to their insight into the universality of their origin and the centralization of their psychic forces, tend to forget or to deny the meaning of individuality, in order to escape the painful consequences of self-responsibility and its problems. Westerners, on the other hand, are inclined to over-rate their individuality while forgetting their universal origin, which alone can give meaning to this individuality. Both extremes are one-sided and misleading.

The first extreme leads to a falling back into consciouslessness (which, indeed, avoids all suffering, but also the very meaning of existence), already expressed in the ancient Indian ideal of profound sleep (*turīya*) and the general "deep-sleep speculation." The latter extreme leads to a clinging to material things and an identification with the body, and finally to death and destruction.

The Buddha seems to have been the first to have opposed the doctrine of "deep sleep" with the ideal of complete awakening of consciousness within the individual life (and not as a nebulous and purely negative nirvana): a state of awakening he not only proclaimed, but also demonstrated in his own life. He therefore recognized the necessity and the meaning of rebirth, that is, the continuity of consciousness until its full unfoldment and maturity by realizing its highest intensity and completeness in the individual experience of universality.

The enormous distance and tension between the individual and the universal, the ephemeral and the eternal, the innermost concentration and the all-inclusive vision, are bridged in that spiritual form, which, as Goethe says, develops in life, and cannot be destroyed by any power of the world once it has been created and has become conscious reality. Seen from here, the meaning of inner vision in Tibetan meditation, in which the creative symbol to which we aspire takes on spiritual form, is that instead of a stillborn intellectual abstraction, we have the inspiration of a direct experience.

The principle of effective form is that the force we observe already in the material-organic phase of biological development is a meaningful and order-creating principle, which creates from the elementary, yet unformed material a self-preserving and self-perpetuating organism. In other words, it is a creative principle that, in spite of the changing constituents of the organism it creates, contains an inherent directive or form-preserving urge, which embodies itself again and again until it succeeds in creating so perfect a form that it becomes conscious of itself.

As an example, we may be reminded of the miraculous faculty of the human body to assimilate the most incongruous types of matter, be it in the form of inorganic or organic substances, and to transforming them into the particular body and mind of the personality whose organism incorporates these various materials. It is as if a central, but unconscious force were using these various materials like bricks to build up a predetermined form according to spiritual and physical conditions.

We see the same principle in all organic forms of life; they reproduce exactly the preceding organism. The simplest organism reproduces itself by division, thus it knows no death and is quasi-immortal. But it pays for this immortality with either lack of consciousness or with a very limited one. On the other hand, with progressive centralization of consciousness, death occurs. Death, in other words, is the sign of higher development, and if it happens consciously, it offers a different kind of immortality, which is achieved by entering a greater unit than the one created by the process of individuation. It is the establishment of universality, the recognition of a greater life, beyond the range of the individual.

"There is," according to Edmund W. Sinnott, a distinguished biologist,

> much further evidence now, especially from the plants, that every cell of an organism has within it the potentiality to make a whole, though this rarely can be realized after the cell has progressed beyond its early stages. While it still possesses this potentiality however, it does not exercise it but subordinates itself to the developing pattern, which the whole mass of cells is forming, and takes its proper place within it. What it will become depends on where it is. The same tendency to move toward a single whole is shown in other ways.[2]

In fact, our individual consciousness is the stepping-stone toward a universality and world-openness, which does not destroy the achievements of our personality, but rather enlarges them. A cell, subordinating itself to the greater organism, does not lose its individuality, but rather enhances it, because it partakes of the higher achievements of the organism in which it functions. The more our consciousness persists in its own individuality, and the less it sees the complete whole of which it is a part, or which it reflects, the more real is its death. "Constancy and conservatism are qualities of the lifeless, not the living. In a similar fashion, psychical activity is creative."[3]

Creativity, however, means to add a new dimension to the already known or experienced. In this way, we combine change with constancy, a possibility that was overlooked in the Hindu religions of India but is the basis of Taoism and its predecessor, the I Ching, in which change appears as transformation. Transformation is change according to law, instead of random change, which would be unforeseeable, unavoidable, and destructive, because it would render any intelligent purpose or any goal impossible. Whether a goal is reached or not is irrelevant; the main thing is that it gives direction. Direction is of supreme importance in Buddhism, as in practically all systems of thought, whether religion, philosophy, or science.

A human being without direction is a being without character, because character is what gives a human being direction. It is, therefore, why the teachings of the Buddha are a Way of Life, which has to be trodden in a certain direction. For this reason, one who has attained unshakable insight in the nature of the Way is called a *sotapan*, or "One Who has Entered the Stream" moving in one direction, i.e., one who has found his aim and moves irresistibly towards it. He may be the lowest of the eight Noble Disciples, but he is one of the Perfect Ones (or Holy Ones), who never can regress or fall into the lower states of life, because he is in conformity with the laws of life, either on account of faith, conviction, or profound insight into the nature of things (dharma). (For more on this subject refer to my *Psychological Attitude of Early Buddhist Philosophy*.)[4]

Therefore, the conditions for winning the stream (*sotāpattiyanga*) are said to be companionship with the wise, hearing the Dharma, wise consideration, and conformity with the universal law. This directiveness is even found in all processes of nature, as is recognized in expressions like *bhavanga-sota*, the subconscious stream of life, from which consciousness arises if there is resistance to the ever-moving stream or a slowing down of its movement, because any kind of thought activity tries to arrest this flow by dividing its different phases, by defining and thus limiting them or isolating them in time.

"Here it is necessary to see clearly the relation between this universal goal-seeking quality of organisms, inherent in their living stuff, and the influence environment exerts on the nature of the goals that are being sought."[5] To think that the progress of life-forms was caused and ensured through a kind of competition, or the survival of the fittest (which may have been a principle of commercial or industrial England during Darwin's lifetime), might be a reasonable and logical conclusion, but it is not confirmed by nature, where obsolete forms often persist a long time after their usefulness is exhausted or conditions of existence have changed.

In fact, the form principle is so strong that every organism tries to perpetuate its form, irrespective of the material from which it is built. "Form makes the particles, not particles the form," as Sinnott says,[6] and, as we may add, the shape of the bricks does not determine the style of the house. With the same bricks, you can form a castle or a hut, a palace or a factory. Therefore, I say that form is more important than content, because form determines the content or the matter from which it is composed. Even the most valuable material is useless if it is not formed; and vice versa, the most ordinary material becomes valuable if it is formed. Ordinary clay, given the right form, can become a priceless work of art or a useful object.

The moment an organism becomes a conscious individual through centralization and unification of all its functions and qualities, such that it represents a whole in which all parts are subordinated to one purpose, it becomes an independent center of consciousness and, due to this centralization, a focus of forces that are able not only to influence other organisms, but also to maintain their own continuity until complete maturity and fulfillment or perfection is achieved. From a dark unconscious drive develops conscious striving for individual consciousness in its greatest intensity. "The insistent tendency among living things for bodily development to reach and maintain, as a norm or goal, an organized living system of a definite kind, and the equally persistent directiveness, or goal-seeking, that is the essential feature of behavior, and thus finally the basis of all mental activity, are fundamentally the same thing, merely two aspects of the basic regulatory character all living stuff displays."[7]

The transformation from an unconscious urge, or dark drive of merely instinctive action, toward reflective consciousness, or a clear (not merely instinctive) thought that is independent of inner drives, is, as C. G. Jung says, a second cosmogony. Reflective consciousness enables the human being to become conscious of itself and of the world in which it lives, allowing it to step from the animal-like collective consciousness of inherited biological instincts into the realm of responsibility and decision as a separate individual. The creative consciousness of spiritual vision deals not only with a given world; through the fire of personal experience, it enables the converting of the given material into a meaningful cosmos, in which the individual forms itself into a fully conscious expression of the universe. Both reflective consciousness and creative consciousness are of vital importance.

At the step of complete individuation, consciousness becomes an effective, self-perpetuating center; but only in the stage of creative vision is the form of mind being achieved that not only guarantees continuity beyond the respective incarnation, but also gives meaning and direction to it. Only such a formed and form-creating consciousness is what we call mind. All human beings have the gift of consciousness, but not all can be called spiritual. Though consciousness is the precondition and basis of spirituality, it is not identical with it. Only when the consciousness becomes creative does it become spiritual and, as such, at the same time formed by experience. It achieves a form, which like a seed has the capacity of transformation and carries in itself the quality of life and growth.

What we see today in the simile of the seed shows again how the similar pictures, the similar archetypal symbols, surface again in all religious forms of expression and how these forms actually tell us more than any purely scientific or mathematical statement which, though it is more precise and objective, leaves out the essential, namely the incommensurable moment of dynamism, the transformation, which is characteristic of all life. This property is shared by the mind and the symbol, and therefore the latter is the means consciousness uses to penetrate the realm of the spirit and to become finally itself living and imperishable spirit, which in spite of all transformations and incarnations ripens toward maturity and completeness.

In the presence of meditative vision, the form creation of the mind takes place, a form creation that survives all transformations and determines their process and direction, thus bridging past and future and making them into the timeless body of an all-inclusive present.

Teilhard de Chardin experienced such a vision—in which the Mass became an experience of cosmic proportions—in the Ordos Desert. The description of this Mass convinced me immediately that Teilhard de Chardin, as no thinker before him, saw clearly the future of humanity and the way toward the realization of this future.

It is strange, but perhaps all the more meaningful, that this experience came to him in the Ordos Desert, in the cultural space of Mongolia, where until recently a form of Tibetan Buddhism prevailed. We are dealing here with a realm of consciousness in which the Eucharistic idea lived in a form hardly known in the West, yet one so similar to the Eucharistic Christianity that we can only wonder how, in two different places of the world and from entirely different preconditions, a similar idea could arise. Even formerly, when the historical development of Buddhism in Tibet was still unknown, a theory existed that here perhaps early Christian influences were at work; and this idea was strengthened by the impression of the first Jesuits who came to Lhasa, in the year 1750. They were surprised by the similarity between the Buddhist rituals and Christian Eucharistic ideas and rituals.

Now, we know from the history of Buddhism that Christianity had no influence upon the development of Buddhism, but that the idea of transubstantiation of matter and the spiritual transformation of humans and word in the act of religious devolution existed long before contact with Christianity was established and already had been connected with a ritual, which was very similar to that of Christianity. This fact only shows that we are dealing with realities of the human spirit, which can be discovered and experienced at all times, by those who penetrate into this realm.

Perhaps you are familiar with the mantric formula *Oṁ Maṇi Padme Hūṁ*. It is generally interpreted in a very superficial manner as "the dewdrop in the Lotus," which sounds very poetical, but has little to do with the real meaning, as far as this can be expressed in simple words. The mantra expresses that the jewel (mani) of divine reality must be realized in the lotus-like vessel (padma) of our own heart. Teilhard de Chardin says this in a similar way and in almost identical terms: "My chalice and my paten are in the depth of a soul, which is wide open to all forces, which in one moment rise from all points of the earth (world) and converge upon the spirit."[8]

What has happened in these few words is so wonderful that I feel that they could only be those of a man who had gone through an experience of profound vision and clarity of mind. Here we have a definition and a clear picture. The human mind, the whole consciousness, converges towards the spirit, when all forces and qualities of the individual and its surroundings converge toward completeness within it.

Here is shown, what really should be understood by "spirit." Nowadays, so much is being said about "mind," "spirit," and "spiritual things" that we have lost sight of the actual meaning of this word. The "spirit" can arise in consciousness only when there is a creative force, which connects all factors of life and consciousness and thus makes them into a unity.

What appears to me so extraordinary is that this Mass goes beyond all ordinary theological concepts and ideas, and becomes a hymn to the universe, and in this way the totality of the universe, as the celebrant experiences it, is given as an offering:

> All the things of the world which this day will bring increase; all those that will diminish; all those that will die: all of them, Lord, I try to gather into my arms, so as to hold them out to you in offering. This is the material of my sacrifice; the only material you desire. . . . Receive, O Lord, this all-embracing host, which your whole creation, moved by your magnetism, offers you at this dawn of a new day.[9]

He calls this offering "the offering of the totality of all mundane endeavor that has been collected in the heart."[10] It could not have been said more perfectly.

Here I would like to quote a parallel statement, written by a Buddhist writer and saint in the eighth century of our era. His name was Śāntideva, and the statement is to be found in his famous treatise "The Way Toward Enlightenment" (*Bodhicāryāvatāra*). He speaks on dedication and sacrifice, and summarizes his thoughts in this beautiful prayer:

> In order to take possession of the jewel of enlightenment, I worship the Blessed Ones and the stainless jewel of their teachings, as well as the spiritual sons of the Enlightened Ones, the oceans of virtues. Whatever there is in this world in the way of flowers, herbs and life-giving waters or mountains of precious stones or forest solitudes for meditation, of creepers with perfumed colorful blossoms, of trees whose branches are bent under the load of precious fruit, of lovely lotus ponds which can reverberate from the song of swans; in short, all that can serve

as an offering and what is contained in the infinity of space and belongs to nobody—I can collect it in my mind and lay it at the feet of the Blessed Ones and their spiritual sons. I am without any merit and therefore poor; I have nothing with which I could worship them. May the Enlightened Ones, who have no other thought than the welfare of others, may they accept these gifts for my sake."

Returning to Teilhard de Chardin, let us hear what further he has to say: "Now, O Lord, through the conscription of the world, we gain the luster and perfume of the universe." When I read these words, the remembrance rises in my mind of a beautiful Japanese picture representing the cosmic Buddha Amitābha, who in a gigantic form rises over the horizon of a vast landscape. Here, too, we see the cosmic description of an inner experience.

If we were to regard these things as being merely the expression of poetic fantasy, we would miss the real meaning of such symbolical representations, because here we are not in the realm of the poetical or the aesthetical, but in what has been experienced deeply and is connected with the whole tradition of Eastern religiosity.

And now comes the last and greatest sacrifice, beyond that which we mentioned in the lines from Śāntideva. After the praying one has opened his heart to the Enlightened Ones and has offered himself as their tool (similar to St. Francis, who said, "Lord, make me an instrument of thy peace"), he renounces the fruits of his devotion and his good works, and promises to devote himself to all living beings, instead of working for his own salvation. In other words, he prefers to share the sufferings of his fellow beings in order to be an active helper toward their liberation, rather than resting content on the pedestal of his own achievements. And thus he vows, "Whatever merit I may have gained, may I become on account of it a soother of other's sufferings."

Teilhard de Chardin also, as we have shown, speaks of the offerings of the totality of the endeavors of all living beings. Here we have an exact parallel to Śāntideva's thoughts. Furthermore, Teilhard de Chardin says,

> What my heart wishes, in its inappropriate desire, that you are giving me in great measure always, so that the beings not only should exist in solidarity among each other and depend on each other, so that none could exist without the others who surround them, and depend on the same centre that a real life, to whom they all are subject, gives them their consistence and unification.[11]

Here also, the desire for liberation becomes the desire for the liberation of all.

What is this center, from which all beings depend? As you well know, the Buddha never defined the Godhead. We have noted before that the Buddha after his enlightenment never spoke about God. It seems to me that the ones who have experienced the highest, or in our language, "have experienced God," cannot talk about it any more, because they have realized the insufficiencies of all words. So long as we try to define, so long as the word still means some form of discrimination, we are taking something away from the experience that goes beyond all concepts and can be realized only in silence.

The silence of the Buddha was more significant than all our words. It was the silence of the ultimate inexpressible mystery that is open to all, but which must be approached by each single person alone. It is the mystery of that center all human beings share, in which the whole universe is contained.

This center is all-comprehensive depth consciousness, in which the sum total of all experiences and all forms of life of the begin-

ningless and endless circle of all events of the universe is accumulated. It is called in Buddhist terminology "the treasure-house of
consciousness" (*ālaya-vijñāna*), and in this center the solidarity of
all beings is contained. It is the source of all creative forces.

Without reaching this center, we cannot find liberation. But
because this center contains the solidarity of all living beings, we
cannot liberate ourselves without sharing this liberation with all
humanity, as I think Christ has already demonstrated. The light of
God would be what in Buddhism we call "the consciousness of
enlightenment" (*bodhicitta*), which consists in becoming conscious
individually of that universal center within us.

Let us hear again, what Teilhard de Chardin has to say in this
connection:

> Rich with the sap of the world, I rise up towards the spirit whose
> vesture is the magnificence of the material universe but who
> smiles at me from beyond all victories; and lost in the mystery
> of the flesh of God, I cannot tell which is the more radiant bliss:
> to have found the Word and to be able to achieve mastery over
> matter, or to have mastered matter and so be able to attain and
> submit to the light of God. . . .
>
> I firmly believe that everything around me is brought about
> by that marvelous diaphany which causes the luminous warmth
> of a single life to be objectively discernible in and to shine forth
> from the depth of every event, every element![12]

What he says here has, again, a profound parallel especially
in Tantric Buddhism of the Vajrayāna ("the Diamond Vehicle,"
prevalent in Tibet): "The secret of the divine flesh" corresponds
with what in the terminology of Buddhism would be called the
Nirmāṇakāya, the "body of transformation." And this Nirmāṇakāya,
again, is an emanation of the inspirational body (Sambhogakāya)

and the Dharmakāya, the universal body, which in the deeper sense is the body of us all.

The creative and inspirational force of the Sambhogakāya, however, is the source of all the mantric words. To have found the "word" is equivalent to the discovery of the mantric way, through which we become masters over all that has become (the realm of matter) and so transform and dissolve it in the divine light of the origin. The "word" meant here is not the communicating word; it has nothing to do with cybernetics or with concepts of what we understand philologically as a word. It has to do with the creative word, which in the Gospel of St. John is called "logos," and is what was originally meant by this term.

If we speak of "logos" nowadays, we associate this term with operations of discursive thought and with the intellect, while the "logos" of which the New Testament speaks, is (if I understand it rightly) the word of power, the unspeakable word, I would say, that can be experienced only within ourselves. It expresses itself in sound symbols, which, like every symbol, are infinitely many-sided and which may have a different meaning on every plane of consciousness. For this reason, it cannot be defined or limited to one meaning—in short, it is the primordial sound, from which everything arises. This mantric word has been lost by the Western world, more or less, and I believe that the East could be of great help to the West in this respect, in reestablishing the value of the mantric word.

Even the Catholic liturgy, which until recently was one for the whole world, has now been translated into the different national languages. I must confess that this change somewhat shocked me. How can one be so blind and deaf to the mantric significance of a liturgy (in which for nearly two millennia the spirit of Christianity was crystallized) as to expect that it could be secularized through an objective philological translation without losing anything spiritually? The unity of Christian culture depends to a great extent on the oneness and generality or the common use of a sacred language, similar to Sanskrit, which is the common sacred language of the Hindus and the majority of Buddhists. Even in a country like Tibet, where Sanskrit is generally unknown and the sacred scriptures of Buddhism had to be translated into Tibetan, all mantric formulas, and especially those of the liturgy, have been left in the original language, namely Sanskrit.

To return to the "mystery of the divine flesh," or body, here again is a profound symbol, which reminds me of a poem by Rainer Maria Rilke. It is entitled "The Buddha in Glory" (the Buddha, surrounded by his aura) and not only represents in its imagery and symbolism a deeply felt Buddhist Tantric view, but also provides an astonishing concordance with Teilhard de Chardin's aforementioned thought. Here is the poem in the beautiful translation by J. B. Leishman:

> Core's core, centre of all circulations,
> almond self-enclosed and sweetening—
> all from here to all the constellations
> is your fruit-pulp: you I sing.

> How released you feel from all belonging!
> In the infinite expands your rind,
> and within it your strong juice is thronging;
> and a radiance from within is kind,

> for those glowing suns of yours are spinning
> on their ways high overhead.
> But in you has had beginning,
> what shall live when they are dead.[13]

I do not know if Teilhard de Chardin knew this poem. If not, the coincidence of his way to express himself is all the more astonishing when he says:

> Rich with the sap of the world I rise up towards the Spirit whose vesture is the magnificence of the material universe but who smiles at me from far beyond all victories; and, lost in the mystery of the flesh of God, I cannot tell which is the more radiant bliss: to have found the Word and to be able to achieve mastery over matter, or to have mastered matter and so be able to attain and submit to the light of God."[14]

If he did not know this poem, it is another proof of the profound parallelism between Teilhard de Chardin's conception of the world and that of Tantric Buddhism, namely to represent the universe, with Rilke, as the "fruit-pulp" of that divine force in our innermost center, which "survives all suns." This center of all centers ("core of all cores") is nothing but the Buddhist *ālaya-vijñāna*, the cosmic or universal depth consciousness, which potentially exists in every living being, but which must first be brought into the light of full consciousness to be realized by and in the individual.

In this light happens, as Teilhard de Chardin so beautifully expresses it, "the wondrous diaphany" that is objectively in the depth of all action and of each element and lets the radiating warmth of one and the same life shine through. Becoming conscious of this diaphany in the process of the ultimate experience of universality and completeness of the divine has also been placed at the center of his philosophy by another thinker of our time, Jean Gebser. In his monumental work, *Ursprung und Gegenwart* (The Ever-Present Origin), Gebser writes:

The undivided ego-free man, who no more sees mere parts but realizes "himself," namely the spiritual form, manhood and worldhood, is conscious of the whole, the diaphainon that lies 'before' all beginning and which shines through everything. . . . Once it was only the disciples of Christ who were able to see the transfiguration of Christ. This diaphanation of the world that happened once, this manifestation of spiritual power that happened once, is not a process of the past.[15]

Indeed, this becoming conscious and the becoming transparent of the whole, is mentioned often in the sacred scriptures of Buddhism (especially those of the Mahayana and the Vajrayāna), as for instance, in the transfiguration of Milarepa, the greatest saint and yogi of Tibet, who lived in the same century as St. Francis of Assisi. It is found also in the Śūrangama Sutra and other well-known texts.

The meditation descriptions of the Tantras show the universality, the spiritualization, and the sanctification of the world even more clearly. The Demchog Tantra says that one should regard oneself and all visible things as a divine mandala, each sound as a mantra, and each thought that arises in the mind as a magic unfolding of the great divine wisdom. The meditating person, however, must see himself or herself in the center of the mandala as the divine figure of perfect Buddhahood, whose realization is the goal. Herewith all accidentals disappear; there is nothing more that is arbitrary or unimportant. The things of the external world combine into a sacred circle, in whose center the body becomes a temple.

The mere fact of being conscious and possessing the spiritual power of creation becomes an indescribable miracle. The visible turns into a symbol of a deeper reality. Or, as Goethe said, "Alles Vergängliche ist nur ein Gleichnis" (all that is transient is only a simile for what is imperishable). The audible turns into a mantra, matter into a manifestation of elementary forces.

As a consequence of a similar experience, Teilhard de Chardin blesses all matter, which reveals the dimensions of the divine and without which we would be inert and unconscious of the world and of ourselves—because we would be without the necessary resistance.

> I bless you, matter, and you I acclaim; not as the pontiffs of science and the moralizing preachers depict you, debased, disfigured—a mass of brute forces and base appetites—but as you reveal yourself to me today, in your totality and your true nature. . . .
>
> Now this soul, whose activity is always a synthesis in itself, eludes the investigations of science, the essential concern of which is to analyze things into their elements and their material antecedents; it can be discovered only by inward vision and philosophic reflection. . . .
>
> The aspect of life which most stirs my soul is the ability to share in an undertaking, in a reality, more enduring than myself; it is in this spirit and with this purpose in view that I try to perfect myself and to master things a little more. When death lays its hand upon me it will leave intact these things, these ideas, these realities which are more solid and more precious than I; moreover my faith in Providence makes me believe that death comes at its own fixed moment, a moment of mysterious and special fruitfulness not only for the supernatural destiny of the soul but also for the further progress of the earth.[16]

However, in order to experience matter and the universe in their totality, we must descend to the source of all consciousness, dive into the primordial source of divine being and becoming, which can happen only in meditation, in inwardness, in the reversal of our direction of view.

What I want, my God, is that by a reversal of my forces (of consciousness) which you alone can bring about, my terror in the face of the nameless changes destined to renew my being be turned into an overflowing joy at *being transformed into you.*[17]

In a similar way, the aim of Mahayana Buddhists is to be transformed into an enlightened one, to become complete, by going the way of the Buddha, instead of worshipping him as a historical personality who lived twenty-five hundred years ago on this earth. Strangely, this goal is also reflected in Teilhard de Chardin's conception of Christ, when he says, "As long as I could see—or dared see—in you Lord Jesus, only the man who lived two thousand years ago, the sublime moral teacher, the friend, the brother, my love remained timid and constrained."[18]

The Buddha we reverence, therefore, is not the historical personality of the man Siddhartha Gautama, but rather the divine qualities that are hidden in each being and became apparent in Gautama Shakyamuni, as well as in innumerable other Enlightened Ones of the past and the future. Even the Buddha of the Pali texts did not refrain from striving after the highest qualities, like love, compassion, sympathetic joy, and equanimity, and he described the state of meditation as a "dwelling in God" (*brahma-vihāra*) or the divine state of mind.

The divine is a living force of direction, which manifests itself in the realm of individuality and takes on the character of personality. But it goes beyond the individual consciousness, since it has its origin in the universal depth consciousness. The individuality takes on the character of personality, since it is realized in the human consciousness. If it were only an abstract idea, it would have no influence on life; and if it were merely an unconscious life force, it would not represent a spiritual value—it would not have a forming influence upon the mind.

The directing force at the bottom of our consciousness and of the total development of organic life is also one of the fundamental thoughts of Teilhard de Chardin. Because of it, everything tends toward an aim, the Omega point, or, as in the case of Buddhism, toward the state of enlightenment and completeness.

This directedness or aim-consciousness moving toward a definite goal is, as we pointed out at the beginning of this essay, fundamentally different from Darwin's theory of evolution and the more and less Darwinistic sciences of nature, which on the one hand take their support from the law of causality. Yet, due to the inexplicable converging of causally unconnected lines of events meeting with an unknown inner structure of total world organism, in which our concepts of time and causality lose their meaning, a new factor makes its appearance, for which the materialistic science of the last century could find no better expression than the word "accident." With this word, the happenings, the entire process of the world, will be more or less dismissed as meaningless, while even the remaining, quasi-isolated exceptions are products of chance.

As Sinnott says in *The Biology of the Spirit*:

The hardest blow that Darwin struck at faith was not the proof that man had come from beasts but the assumption that the whole evolutionary process depends finally on variations that arise by chance. A living organism, however, is not a chance-creation but a well-regulated system. It draws random matter and endows it with order and directedness. To see purpose in the lifeless universe may need the eye of faith, but life, at least, evidently moves towards goals. . . . The very existence of spiritual qualities in man suggests that they are manifestations in him of something like them in the universe outside.[19]

Darwin's theory of chance is certainly the weakest point in his otherwise ingenious idea. The word "chance" has, however, a double meaning—not only that of a purely accidental occurrence, but also that of an opportunity! But in order to make use of an opportunity, it is necessary to have an aim-directed impulse, a creative idea, a judging mind, or a persisting form tendency and directedness. This tendency seems inherent in all living things; it is the tendency or the impulse toward the most perfect unfoldment of all potentialities contained in a particular form of life. But since every form of life rests on a beginningless past and thus has the totality of the universe as its basis, the most perfect aim can only be the universal whole.

Development consists therefore not in a progress ad infinitum (or the idea that any further stage is necessarily better than the previous one), but rather in a process of unfoldment of inherent qualities, like the process of growing from the seed to the blossom, during which every stage has its own beauty and justification. In a conscious being, the potentiality exists, sleeping in the darkness of the depth consciousness, until it is awakened and becomes a conscious reality. In human beings, the universe becomes conscious of itself; in terms of theology, becoming conscious is the awakening of the divine in the individual, the awakening of the individual to its universality.

To speak more about the force of direction, where shall we direct ourselves? As I already mentioned, we try to penetrate from the three dimensions of Euclidean space (which we imagine "outside") into a new dimension, and since we cannot find another dimension outside ourselves, the only possibility is to reverse the direction of our search by trying to realize our inner center.

Western psychology now also has made the discovery that human consciousness is more than what we usually take it to be, namely our intellect, our thinking, etc. Unfortunately, however,

modern thinkers have degraded the all-embracing depth consciousness to the "unconscious"—and have thereby declared it to be the
enemy of all reason and the dark source of all uncontrolled drives –
in order to dedicate themselves all the more to the limited surface
consciousness of the intellect. This approach is concerned merely
with the ephemeral interests of our momentary existence, thus losing the connection with all living depth, the center of all centers,
and the source of all divine forces.

The effect has been particularly disastrous in the arts, whether
poetry, painting, sculpture, or music. Most poetry makes no sense,
and painting is either the outcome of chance, a merely accidental
jumble of colors, without the backbone of a proper design or
knowledge of drawing or psychology; the public is deceived by
high-sounding titles of mysterious designations and aesthetical or
philosophical explanations, while in fact the artist sat before the
canvas without having anything to convey, guided only by accidental color effects and forms. The less understandable, the better—the
artist can always resort to the "unconscious," or similar mysterious
forces, to justify the creation. The same holds for sculpture and
music, though a greater amount of technical knowledge is required
and less is left to chance.

The same lack of direction and a consequent uneasiness is
found in modern psychiatry. With all C. G. Jung's merits, which
he acquired in the exploration of depth consciousness (and for this
we cannot be grateful enough), he unfortunately did not dare to
break from the negative formulation of Freud toward a positive
evaluation of depth consciousness and free himself from the ambig-
uous situation into which retaining Freud's one-sided (but fundamental) concepts led him. Though I have often pointed out this
hindrance of modern psychology (I did so as well in my lectures at
the Jung Institute in Zurich), I would like to mention it again,

especially in connection with Teilhard de Chardin's conception of the world.

Words of criticism already have been uttered from different quarters, and I will mention only a few of them, to show that we already have become conscious of this controversial concept of modern psychology. For instance, the Swiss psychiatrist Medard Boss says,

> It is no secret any more that the honored root-concept of modern psychology, the Unconscious, is a very uncritical and dark concept. On top of it, we objectify through this concept involuntary from the outset an important part-phenomenon of the human being, into a vague, impersonal, demonic-anonymal, strata-like thing and give it a merely intellectual, hypostatic construction for the really existing thing.[20]

Jean Gebser writes in a similarly critical way:

> The modern psychological terminology which in contrast to the consciousness postulates an "unconscious" is herewith guilty of a falsification of the originally given psychosomatic facts. This terminology and the strongly structured phenomena that result from this are a classical example of the misconceptions which originate from a radically pursued dualism. The so-called "unconscious" does not exist. There are only different kinds of consciousness.[21]

And now the statement of an English thinker, Alan Watts:

> The modern thinking suffers from a strange preconceived idea, namely that the consciousness is only a superficial outcropping of reality and that the more fundamental we find the power or

the principle or the substance, the more blind and unconscious it must be.[22]

Medard Boss elaborates:

The modern psychology of the Unconscious could in fact be only the first dawn before the awakening, and it is possible that we have seen in the works of C. G. Jung already a ray of the sun. Even the mere use of the term "the unconscious" shows how little Westerners know of the reality of the central consciousness.[23]

Indeed, a Teilhard de Chardin was necessary to make us see the fundamental role of consciousness, and even more, to restore in us the idea of a conscious universe, in which even what we call matter is only another dimension of life, a dimension that appears to us as matter because resistance, form, visibility, and the like have been simply defined as matter. In what else does matter consist, if not in our sense perceptions? In reality, we cannot even touch matter; we can only feel resistance, see forms, describe feelings of touch, experience smells, or register various tastes. But that is not yet matter; it is a number of sense impressions from which we construct the concept of matter. We, therefore, can speak of a material or physical universe only in a very relative sense and related only to our narrowly circumscribed sense perceptions.

With this knowledge, an essential difference between facts of inner and outer space already has been removed, and after, so to speak, the solid ground of an external world has been pulled away from under our very feet, we can approach all the more confidently the inner world, which is so much nearer to us. Unfortunately, we regard the contents of this world only in the mirror of the subconscious, that is, in passively accepted functional effects, consisting of dreams and archetypal symbols that modern psychologists regard as an effect of compelling drives to which the individual is submitted.

The psychology of "drives" is a typical product of a science that is addicted to causality, which may have its justification in the realm of mechanics, but which flounders in the realm of psychic phenomena. Even from the biological point of view, the theory of subconscious drives has been shaken, as the following remarks by Sinnott may show:

> Common experience looks on the idea that we are pushed about by such inner drives as unreal and artificial. What meaning can it have, we say, for men whose lives are dedicated to the pursuit of knowledge or the creation of beauty or the service of their fellows? What place in it is there for devotion and sacrifice and that endless striving for truth and human betterment, which ever distinguished man at its best? How can it satisfy all those who have, burning in their hearts, the flame of divine discontent that lifts men higher than the beasts? Men seem not to be pushed into the finest things they do but to follow the urgent call of something that draws them on through hardship and uncertainty and discouragement to the attainment of a high desire. . . .
>
> This conception has the advantage over the present psychological orthodoxy in that its attitude is forward, towards a goal to be reached, and not back to the push and drive of circumstance, and is true in harmony with the common verdict of experience.[24]

The aim, however, is the becoming complete, in which the consciousness of human beings is as much concerned as their super-individual depth consciousness, in which intuition and reason are combined so that the turning toward that hidden treasury of universal experience is not a blind aimless taking hold of, or a compulsory being overwhelmed by, accidentally upwelling contents of experience, but rather an integral event, in which our individual existence finds its universal fulfillment.

Instead of being content with raising fragmentary impressions of inessential details from the contents of the depth consciousness into the glaring light of the intellect and exposing them to a deadly dissecting analysis, we must turn our conscious mind inward, in order to transform the potential forces of the depth into active ones. In other words, instead of raising the archetypal symbols and visions from the depth to the surface of consciousness and exposing them to conceptual thought or the triviality of mundane purposes and aims, we should turn the focus of our individual consciousness upon its universal source, by which we shall awaken to the Greater Life and to a synthesis of our spirit.

The way toward this awakening of the spirit or the perfect enlightenment is not to be measured in lifetimes; it comprises world periods and universal perspectives, as only a scholar of the nature of Teilhard de Chardin could visualize and put into words. From the point of view of this spiritual perspective, he could say, "For those, however, who see the synthesis of the spirit continuing on earth beyond their own brief existence, every event is charged with interest and promise."[25]

This synthesis of the spirit on the axis of time corresponds to the axis of spatial extension—in the knowledge that each individual consciousness is not closed in itself or limited, but penetrates other similar centers and is itself pervaded by the affects of other conscious centers. In this way, space and time become dimensions of consciousness. Therefore, Teilhard de Chardin says,

> The overwhelming vastness of the Cosmos need no longer appall us, since the indefinite layers of Time and Space, far from being the lifeless desert in which we seemed to be lost, show themselves

to be the bosom which gathers together the separate fragments of a huge Consciousness in process of growth. . . .

The consciousness which we are gradually acquiring of our physical relationship with all parts of the Universe presents a genuine enlarging of our separate personalities. It is truly a progressive realization of the universality of the things surrounding each of us. And it means that in the domain external to our flesh, our real and whole body is continuing to take shape.[26]

This understanding corresponds exactly to the Tantric idea of the universe as our greater or spiritual body, as mentioned before. So long as we feel the universe as something alien, which confronts us as an object, we are playthings of forces and are helplessly drifting in the circle of becoming and disintegrating. Thus we experience the universe as samsara. However, the moment we realize the universe is our "greater body" and penetrate it spiritually, we experience the great transformation; we have attained liberation, the state of nirvana.

Tibetan Buddhism speaks of the three mysteries of body, speech, and mind. (For more on this subject, refer to my *Foundations of Tibetan Mysticism*.) The personality of spiritually undeveloped individuals is confined to their material form of appearance, the physical body. The personality of spiritually progressive individuals is no more confined to the material of their form of appearance, but includes also their mental and psychic functions, the body of consciousness, which extends beyond the physical body.

This body of consciousness widens with individuals who live in their ideals and extends beyond the realm of individual interests and experiences into the freedom of universality and living relationships—into the realm of the beautiful, the creative action, aesthetic enjoyment, and intuitive experience. But the enlightened individuals whose consciousness embraces the universe have the universe as their body. They become manifestations of the universal mind, their vision becomes an expression of highest reality and their speech becomes mantric power and sacred wisdom. Here the mystery of body, speech, and mind reveals itself in its true nature, as the three planes of action, in which all spiritual life exists.

Teilhard de Chardin sees this process of realization in the synthesis of these three planes of action and in a convergence of all cosmic tendencies of development toward the focus of a higher consciousness. This is more than a mere sum of all conscious experience, but rather its integration, its highest potential, the ultimate dimension of consciousness, which must be sought far beyond a simple, perfected human collective, in order to be capable of connecting the nerves that extend into the world.

> But if we seek to determine the position and analyze the properties of this Supreme Centre, it soon becomes clear that we must look far beyond and far above any mere aggregation of perfected mankind. If it is to be capable of joining together in itself the prolonged fibers of the world, the apex of the cone within which we move can be conceived only as something that is ultra-conscious, ultra-personalized, ultra-present. It must reach and act upon us, not only indirectly, through the universal network of physical synthesis, but also, and even more directly from the centre (that is to say from consciousness to consciousness) by touching the most sensitive in ourselves.[27]

Seen from this elevated standpoint, we understand Teilhard de Chardin's profound conviction that "it is the great task of modern man, to create a way forward, in breaking over the threshold of some higher level of consciousness. Whether we are Christian or non-Christian, the people inspired by this particular conviction constitute a homogenous category."[28]

Teilhard de Chardin obviously means us all, whether we are Christians or not. To each one who is conscious of this great task, to each one who strives toward the highest realization of the spirit, Teilhard de Chardin has rendered an immortal service.

Chapter 4

Drugs and Meditation

Consciousness Expansion and Disintegration versus Concentration and Spiritual Regeneration

When people nowadays recommend "consciousness-expanding" drugs as a substitute or an incentive for meditation, they start from the naive preconception that expansion is synonymous with the attainment of higher values. But the mere expansion of a muddled consciousness, in which the faculties of discrimination, mental balance, and understanding have not yet been developed, does not constitute an improvement and will not lead to the attainment or the realization of a higher dimension of consciousness; it will only lead to a worse confusion, to an expansion of ignorance and an indiscriminate involvement in irrelevant impressions and emotions. Therefore, wise persons would rather follow the advice of the great spiritual leaders and benefactors of humanity by concentrating the mind and improving its quality, instead of trying to expand it without rhyme or reason, that is, without having developed the faculty of understanding or discrimination.

The main medium of this so-called consciousness-expansion is LSD, and its prophets who propagate it as a substitute for meditation are characteristically only those who have neither experience nor qualification in the field of meditation. They have never gone

69

through any serious spiritual training, or sadhana, based on millennia of experience and psychological exploration, as handed down and taught by many of the great spiritual traditions of humanity.

In the process of meditation, the gradual achievement of integration, we are not concerned with an "expansion" of consciousness but, as Jean Gebser, one of the most incisive thinkers of our time, rightly says, with an intensification of consciousness:

> The mistake that is made nowadays, and which has its reason in the qualitatively accentuated rational attitude, consists in the opinion that a material "more" must correspond to a "more" in the realm of consciousness. This "more," however, concerns only the reflecting knowledge, which has quantitative character. For this reason alone we had to insist, that we must not fall into the error of striving after consciousness-expansion, but that what matters is a consciousness-intensification. A mere consciousness-expansion leads as much to destruction as the material atomization, which to some extent has already taken shape [or rather *Ungestalt*, its "misshapen form"].[1]

We need only look at modern paintings and drawings of so-called psychedelic art, which appear to be composed out of thousands of fragments, like a smashed and splintered mirror in which the world is reflected and broken up into a chaos of disconnected details, and we will understand what this process of atomization is leading to.

However, the main difference between the states of consciousness caused by LSD and those created by meditation—and here I am not speaking theoretically, but from my own experience—is that LSD totally deprives us of any control: we are so helplessly tossed about by our emotions and deceived by hallucinations or creations of chaotic imagination that our attention is scattered and confused by thousands of fragmentary images and sense impressions. Meditation, on the other hand, is a creative process that converts the chaos of upsurging feelings, thoughts, uncontrolled volitions, and contending inner forces into a meaningful "cosmos" (a harmonized "uni-verse") in which all psychic faculties are centered and integrated in the depth of our consciousness.

Only the creation of this inner center makes us into consciously spiritual beings and lifts us beyond the blind drives of our animal nature that binds us to the chaos of samsara (the world of delusion). LSD, on the other hand, leads away from the center into an ever more fragmentizing multiplicity of unrelated, eternally changing projections of subconscious thought contents, which, though momentarily capturing our attention, leave us as completely passive spectators of a psychic film-show; and the longer we devote ourselves to its contemplation, the surer it will suffocate all creative impulses and all individual effort towards their realization.

In this connection we may remember the words of Goethe: "Was du ererbt von deinen Vätern hast, erwirb es, um es zu besitzen"[2] (What you have inherited from your forefathers, you must earn by your own effort, if you wish to make it your own.) The "inheritance of our forefathers" is in a wider sense the inheritance of our own past and ultimately of the whole universe from which we have emerged, or as Zen Buddhists would have it, "our original face that existed before our parents were born."

This "original face," however, is far from being the face of our already completed or immanent Buddhahood, though it may contain all the potentialities of an enlightened mind. I would rather define it as the reflection of the universal depth consciousness, or in Buddhist terminology, the "store consciousness" (ālaya-vijñāna), which contains the accumulated experiences of all forms of existence, the experiences of an infinite past—in which all possibilities of life are contained, from the lowest to the highest states of consciousness (or from the most primitive to the most universal dimensions of consciousness), from the blind urges of brutish or demoniacal drives and cruel passions to the most beneficial activities of divine or enlightened beings, in whom the unconscious forces and blind passions have been sublimated into clear knowledge, love, and compassion.

To equate this ālaya-vijñāna with the "Buddha Nature" and to believe that merely by suppressing or eliminating our thoughts and aspirations, our volition and discrimination—in short, our whole individuality and our intellectual qualities—we could attain the enlightenment of a Buddha, is a naive belief and an unfounded hypothesis, unsupported by experience and contradicting the entire Buddhist tradition, which is concerned with the sublimation, harmonization, and integration of all human qualities and capabilities. That tradition emphasizes the importance of individual effort (*vīrya* and *vyayama*), consequent religious practice (sadhana), cultivation of creative spiritual qualities (*bhāvāna*), discriminative thought (*dharmavicaya*), clear knowledge and wisdom (prajña), conscious awareness and remembrance (*smṛti*), perfect aspirations (*samyak samkalpa*), consciously directed concentrative meditation (*ekāgratā*), love and compassion for all beings (*maitri* and *karuṇā*), and faith (*śraddhā*) in the enlightened teachers of humanity.

Enlightenment can be gained neither by passively "sitting" nor by violence in the endeavor to suppress human feelings and thoughts or in the desperate struggle for the solution of some paradoxical problem. The key to enlightenment can be found neither in rigid concentration nor in an expansion of consciousness through artificial means.

The mere reduction of the field of spiritual vision to a single point, a single subject, concept, or thought sequence, excluding all other thoughts or sense impressions—corresponding to the exclusiveness of a perspective viewpoint, in which only a one-sided, foreshortened observation of the object is possible—prevents us from observing the organic relationship of our subject with its background as well as with ourselves. This kind of concentration, which is practiced in science and discursive thought, and is based on strict logical laws, is as little suitable to lead to enlightenment as the indiscriminate expansion of consciousness of an untrained, inexperienced person who has neither the knowledge nor the judgment to be able to understand or make use of the phenomena of this expanded consciousness. Such a person is in the same position as a scientifically unprepared and inexperienced person would be if sent into space in a rocket or spacecraft; though the experiences gone through would be the same as those of an astronaut, he or she would return to earth as ignorant as before leaving it, because whatever was seen and experienced could not convey any meaning, but would only lead to confusion, bewilderment, and fear.

Even if the experiences caused by drugs were similar to those experienced in meditation or mystic visions (for which there is not the slightest evidence, because those who are using drugs have no knowledge of real meditation), they would not convey to spiritually untrained persons anything of the deeper meaning of those visions and experiences, because of their inability to interpret the language of psychic symbols and phenomena. They would not be able to establish meaningful relations between themselves (as observers) and the observed phenomena—in other words, between the universal depth consciousness and their individual (peripheral) surface consciousness—because they skipped the way leading from the periphery of the normal waking consciousness to the depth consciousness or their inner center.

The experience of this way, which leads step by step from our surface consciousness into the depth of our mind in the process of meditative absorption, is of paramount importance, because it employs and stimulates all our faculties of thinking, feeling, and intuition. Those who believe they can rely on mere intuition, before they have developed control over the basic functions of their intellect on the level of everyday life experience, will never be able to discern between truth and self-deception.

The mere "expansion" of consciousness therefore has no value unless we have found our inner center, in which all the faculties of mind and psyche are integrated and to which all our experiences are referred as their ultimate judge and arbiter. This inner center is situated between the poles of the individual peripheral consciousness of the intellect and the non-individual depth consciousness in which we partake of the greater life of the universe. When this center functions rightly the whole impression is one of evident harmony with inner life. The inner and the outer exist not against but for each other.

> Always, then, the presence of the basic vital centre is expressed in the easy equilibrium of the two poles and if one preponderates over the other the result is a wrong relation to heaven and earth, to the world and to the self.
>
> Just as failure to achieve the right centre always implies a disturbance of the living whole, so the achievement of it demonstrates nothing less than that state in which the *whole* is kept alive *in the right tension between the two poles*.[3]

The tendency toward centralization is not only a biological and psychological necessity, but a law of universal dynamics, pervading the entire cosmos irrespective of whether applied to spiral nebulae or solar systems, planets or electrons: every movement has a tendency to create its own center or its own axis, as the only possible form of stability within the infinite movement of all that lives.

Where, however, life becomes conscious of itself, a new, subtler centralization takes place in a consciousness that creates its own focus, moving as if it were on an infinite axis from distant past toward an equally distant future (as it appears to us), or more correctly, which moves toward a present that (to us) is in a state of continual transformation.

The universal depth consciousness is common to us all, but what is made out of it, or what is extracted or distilled from it and brought to the surface, depends on the individual. Just as the waters of the ocean contain all kinds of substances in a state of dissolution, in a similar way the universal depth consciousness contains potentially all psychic qualities. From the waters of the ocean, we can extract gold as well as ordinary kitchen salt, depending on the degree of (chemical) concentration and the method employed. In a similar way, it is possible to extract from the universal depth consciousness, either divine or demoniacal forces, life-promoting or life-destroying powers, powers of darkness or of light.

Those who descend into the depth of this universal consciousness without having found their inner center will be swallowed by it or will be swept away to their doom like a rudderless ship lost in the immensity of the ocean. Only to the wise will the depth reveal its treasures. Knowledge and wisdom, however, are founded on patient observation of the laws of existence in the mirror of the stilled mind, in which the inner relations of all things become apparent and our intuitive awareness is brought to fruition.

If, however, intuition does not find also a clear expression in our thoughts, it can have no effective influence on our life, but is dissipated in the fog of vague feelings and dreamlike fantasies and visions, because no force can be effective if it is not formed, i.e., concentrated and directed. On the other hand, thoughts and items of knowledge or truth that have been developed only on the intellectual level have to be verified in life by direct experience in order to become living reality. Only then will they have the power to transform our life and to influence our deepest nature.

Those who only stick to their thoughts remain prisoners of thoughts, just as those who live only in vague forms of intuition become prisoners of their momentary moods and impressions. Those, however, who are able to harmonize the faculties of clear thought and intuition make the best use of both. They will enjoy the freedom of intuition, and at the same time they will be capable of utilizing its results in the creation of a spiritual universe, or *Weltanschauung*, whose structure will be an ever-growing edifice of sublime beauty and transparency, and whose crowing pinnacle will be the radiating jewel of enlightenment, in which the structure will find its completion.

Meditation

The East discovered the eternal recurrence of the same conditions and similar events. The West discovered the value of the uniqueness of each event or existential condition. The East kept its gaze fixed upon the cosmic background, the West on the individual foreground. The complete picture, however, combines foreground and background, integrating them into a higher unity. The complete human being, the person who has become whole (and therefore "holy"), unites the universal with the individual, the uniqueness of the moment with the eternity of the cyclic recurrence of constellations and existential situations.

In the knowledge of immortality the East neglected the mundane life. In the knowledge of the uniqueness and value of the present moment, the West neglected the immortal. Only in the deepest aspects of the Vajrayāna (the mystic school of Tibetan Buddhism), as well as in the I Ching (the oldest book of Chinese wisdom), has the attempt been made to connect the vision of the foreground with that of the background, to connect the momentary with the eternal and the uniqueness of every situation with the ever-recurring constellations of universal forces.

Only those who, while recognizing and understanding their Western inheritance, penetrate and absorb the heritage of the East can gain the highest values of both worlds and do justice to both. East and West are the two halves of our human consciousness, comparable to the two poles of a magnet, which condition and correspond to each other, and cannot be separated. Only if individuals realize this fact will they become complete human beings. Leo Baeck writes, "In man life becomes conscious of itself, and with this it develops into a task and into freedom, so that it can receive anew, make a new start, that it can regain its beginning, its heritage and its origin, and can be reborn."

The life of human beings is suspended between the poles of heaven and earth. Let us retain within us the width of heaven, but let us not forget the earth that bears us. Earth and heaven are the symbols of the finite and the infinite, in which we share equally. It is not our task to choose between these two poles of our existence or to give up the one for the sake of the other, but to recognize their mutual interdependence and to integrate them into our very being. Our problem, therefore, is not an "either-or" but an "as-well-as," because the human being is the center between heaven and earth, where heaven and earth meet.

Wow

For this reason, the Buddha praised human birth as the best, because only in human life do we find the opportunity to realize the Middle Way, which unites heaven and earth and which alone can give meaning to our existence by freeing us from our attachment to the one or the other extreme. Existence means limitation, but limitation in this sense is not synonymous with narrowness and ignorance; rather it consists in the creation of meaningful form, concentration upon essentials, renunciation of all that is superfluous or nonessential, and the giving up or restraining of desires and cravings—a restraint resulting in greater freedom. The wisest person is the one who is able to convey much with few words; the greatest artist is the one who can express the deepest experience in the simplest form. Therefore, it has been said, "Simplicity reveals the master."

In other words, the finite gives meaning to the infinite, because the infinite can express itself only through finite form; and vice versa, where the finite clings to existence for its own sake, without reflecting the infinite, it becomes meaningless and carries the seeds of death within itself.

Uniqueness in time and expression is the preciousness of form. It is precious because it is transient like a flower, which blossoms and wilts and which nevertheless expresses the eternal character of all flowers and all life. It is the preciousness of the moment, in which timeless eternity is present. It is the preciousness of individual form, in which the infinite is revealed.

Therefore, the Buddha silently held up a flower when the pious pilgrim Subhadra wanted to know the quintessence of the Buddha's teaching. The symbol of the flower, which opens itself to the light of heaven while yet being rooted in the earth, belongs to the deepest symbols of the East. The darkness of the earth and the light of heaven, the powers of the depth in which the experiences of an infinite past of aeons of individual life-forms are stored, and the cosmic forces of supraindividual, universal laws are united in the blossom of spiritual unfoldment into conscious form.

The Buddha—like all Enlightened Ones—is represented as sitting on a lotus throne. The lotus is the prototype of all mandalas, of all centralized systems of a spiritual universe of intricate relationships, of all chakras, or psychic centers, in which the chaos of unconscious forces is transformed into a meaningful cosmos and in which individual existence finds its fulfillment in the final realization of Enlightenment, the state of completeness (the state of being entirely whole, which we call "holy").

The purpose of Buddhist meditation, therefore, is not merely to sink back into the "uncreated" state, into a complete tranquilization with a vacant mind; it is not a regression into the "unconscious" or an exploration of the past, but a process of transformation, of transcendence, in which we become fully conscious of the present, of the infinite powers and possibilities of the mind, in order to become masters of our own destiny by cultivating those qualities that lead to the realization of our timeless nature: to enlightenment. Thus, instead of being a contemplation of a past that we cannot change and cannot influence at all any more, meditation serves to sow the seeds of final liberation and to build already *now* the bodies of future perfection in the image of our highest ideals.

To do this, it is not sufficient merely to "spiritualize" our life; what we need is to "materialize" our spirit. To despise matter for the sake of spirit is in no way better than mistaking matter to be the only reality. Novalis once said that the outer world is nothing but the inner world in a state of mystery.[1] If thus we look at the world with the eyes of a poet—that is, with the eyes of the spirit—we shall discover that the simplest material object, nay, anything that is *formed*, be it by man or by nature, is a symbol of a higher reality and a deeper relationship of universal and individual forces than we ever expected. And since these forces are the same ones that make up our consciousness, our inner life, our very soul, the words of Novalis are no poetic exaggeration, but a profound truth. We have become accustomed to associating the word "matter" with something low and valueless in contrast to what we call "spiritual" and have deprived ourselves because of this one-sided "spirituality" of the very means to penetrate to the core of reality and to give meaning to our life, to our individual existence in this material world. We have torn apart the profound unity between the inner and the outer world by declaring the one to be spiritual and the other to be merely material and in the last resort illusory.

The special function of meditation is to reunite the inner and the outer world, instead of renouncing the one for the sake of the other. Meditation is not an escape from the world, but a means to look deeper into it, unhampered by prejudices or by the familiarity of habit, which blinds us to the wonders and the profound mysteries that surround us. In both philosophy and religion the concepts of oneness, of universality, infinity, boundlessness, formlessness, emptiness, changelessness, timelessness, eternity, and similar one-sided abstractions of a purely conceptual type became the summum bonum and the hallmark of an intellectual spirituality, which tried to isolate them from their counterpoles, namely diversity, individuality, form, materiality, movement in time and space, change, growth, transformation, etc., which were depreciated and scorned as qualities of a lower order and as a negation of ultimate reality. This approach is a typical example of mere word-thinking and logical ratiocination, which is as far from an understanding of reality— or let us say, from the nature of reality, which may have many dimensions—as the attempt to isolate the positive pole from the negative pole of an electric or magnetic field. We may break a piece of magnetized steel as often as we like, but we shall never be able to separate the positive pole from the negative pole; each fragment will always have both. Polarity is an aspect of unity, not an arbitrary duality, but an inseparable whole.

Our abstract thinkers, however, want to have unity without diversity, infinity without anything finite, eternity without change, universality without individuality, emptiness without form, substance without quality, energy without matter, and mind without body, without realizing that unity is meaningless without diversity, or infinity without the finite—that universality cannot be experienced except in the individual and that the individual derives its meaning and value from the realization of its universal background and interrelationship. In other words, universality and individuality are not mutually exclusive or irreconcilable opposites, but the inseparable poles or aspects of the same reality.

We cannot attain to universality by negating or destroying individuality. Individuality, however, is not identical with egocentricity. We are all individuals, but we are not necessarily all egoists. By overcoming our ego we do not lose our individuality; on the contrary, we enrich and widen our individuality, which thus becomes the expression of a greater and more universal life. So long as the illusion of a permanent, unchangeable, separate egohood exists, we oppose ourselves to the very nature of life, because life means movement, change, growth, transformation, unfoldment, and integration into ever more meaningful forms of relationship. By seeing the world from the perspective of our limited little ego and our ephemeral aims and desires, we not only distort it, but make it a prison that separates us from our fellow beings and from the very sources of life. But the moment we become truly selfless by emptying ourselves of all ego tendencies, of our power hunger and all possessiveness and craving, we break down the walls of our self-created prison and become conscious of the immensity and boundlessness of our true being—a being that comprises the infinite forms and potentialities of life and conscious awareness, in which each form represents a momentary constellation of forces and aspects in the continuous stream of life. The fact that no form or aspect of life is a self-contained, unchangeable unit, but exists only in relationship to others and ultimately to the totality of all that exists, is hinted at by the Buddhist term *śūnyatā*, which literally means "emptiness"— empty of self-nature, permanence, or enduring substance.

This emptiness, however, cannot be realized without being conscious of its opposite pole, without realizing form, nor can the function of form be realized without emptiness. (I speak of the "function" of form, because form is not static.) Just as objects can only exist in space and space can only be conceived in relation to objects (or in relation to a "subject"), in the same way form and emptiness condition and penetrate each other. They coexist insepa-rably, for which reason śūnyatā has aptly been circumscribed by the expression "plenum-void," the all-containing, all-producing empti-ness. In its deepest metaphysical sense, it is the primordial ground, the ever-present starting point of all creation. It is the principle of unlimited potentiality, which can be experienced only in moments of complete, unconditioned freedom, moments of spontaneous insight, in which we are lifted out of the net of cause and effect and find ourselves faced with a sense of pure being.

On the intellectual plane śūnyatā is the relativity of all things and conditions, insofar as no thing exists independently in itself, but only in relationship with others and ultimately in relationship to the whole universe. This relationship is more than a mere causal, time-space relationship; it is one of a common ground and of a simultaneous presence of all factors of existence, though certain factors may take a momentary precedence over others. Thus śūnyatā is not "nothingness" but rather "no-thing-ness," though it is the beginning and the end of all things. If we want to make śūnyatā an experience instead of a mere concept of relativity (useful as this may be from the standpoint of philosophical understand-ing), we must consciously go through in meditation the process of creation and dissolution, of becoming and dissolving and reinte-grating. We must *experience* that form is emptiness and emptiness is form, by consciously creating form, until it is visible to the inner eye and filled with life and significance, in order to reabsorb it again bit by bit and stage by stage into śūnyatā, the all-embracing inner space. The process of meditation is dual; it does not consist merely in the reversal of the creative process or in the negation of form, but contains both form creation and form dissolution, because śūnyatā can never become a living experience unless we have realized both poles of its incommensurable nature.

As D. T. Suzuki rightly says, to understand śūnyatā in its deepest sense, "One must experience sitting at the center of existence and viewing things from this hub." To get to the hub of existence, into the center of our being, we must reverse the direction of our mental outlook and turn inward. This turning about in the depth of our consciousness, called *pāravritti*, is the main purpose of all meditation. For long we have looked from within outward, scattering our attention upon the self-created objects of our sense awareness and our mental activities. Now we reverse the direction and go back the way we came, untying the knots by which we have tied ourselves to our present human existence.

The Buddha, according to the Śūrangama Sutra, explained this process by tying a knot into a silk handkerchief, holding it up, and asking Ananda, his favorite disciple, "What is this?"[2] Ananda replied, "A silk handkerchief in which you have tied a knot." The Buddha thereupon tied a second knot in it, and a third one, and continued doing so until he had tied in this way six knots. And each time he asked Ananda what he saw, and each time Ananda replied in the same way.

Thereupon, the Buddha said: "When I tied the first knot, you called it a knot; when I tied the second and third, etc., you still maintained the same answer." Ananda, not comprehending what the Buddha was driving at, became puzzled and exclaimed, "Whether you tie a single knot or a hundred knots, they always remain knots, though the handkerchief is made of variously colored silk threads and woven into a single piece."

The Buddha admitted this, but he pointed out that, though the piece of silk was one and all the knots were knots, there was one difference, namely the order in which they were tied.

To demonstrate this subtle and yet important difference, the Buddha asked how these knots could be untied. And at the same time he started pulling at the knots here and there in such a way that the knots, instead of being loosened, became tighter, whereupon Ananda replied: "I would first try to find out how the knots were tied."

The Buddha exclaimed: "Right you are, Ananda! If you wish to untie a knot you must first find out how the knot was tied. For he who knows the origin of things knows also their dissolution. But let me ask you another question: Can all the knots be untied at the same time?"

"No, Blessed Lord. Since the knots were tied one after another in a certain order, we cannot untie them unless we follow the reverse order."

The Buddha then explained that the six knots correspond to the six sense organs through which our contact with the world is established.

In a similar way, meditation must begin from the level of our present state of existence, of which our body is the most obvious manifestation. Instead of getting entangled in beliefs and opinions, theories and dogmas, spiritual ideas and high-flown hypotheses, we have to untie the knots of our body and mind. We have to relax our tensions and stresses and establish a state of perfect harmony and balance. To establish this balance, our body must be centered and effortlessly resting in itself. Only if our body is centered and all its functions are at rest, can our mind become centered so that we can attain a state of concentration, the first prerequisite of meditation. Concentration should not mean an intellectual effort toward the solution of a problem, but rather a resting of our mind within its own center of gravitation, which is revealed and activated by the interest aroused by the subject of contemplation.

"Interest" means to be within it (*inter-esse*), not to look at it merely from without, but to identify ourselves with it—which is possible only if the subject of our meditation inspires us. But what can we identify ourselves with? Certainly not with an abstract idea, a mere concept, a moral principle, or a philosophical thesis, but only with an ideal embodied in human beings and capable of being realized by human beings. Here is where the image of the perfected human being, the perfectly Enlightened One, the Buddha (or as we may say, the model of the Complete Human Being) comes in. Therefore, at the beginning of the path of meditation an element of devotion, faith in the higher qualities (or the divine nature) of the human being, and dedication to a supreme ideal are the main forces that carry us along toward final realization. Those who believe meditation can be practiced without this faith are indulging in mere acrobatics of the intellect, but they will never penetrate into the realm of the spirit.

Devotion removes the main hindrance of meditation, the ego, and opens us toward a greater life, while inspiration draws us toward the realization of our aim. Without establishing a comprehensive and convincing aim of meditational practice, meditation cannot succeed. For this reason, we have first to state our aim and convince ourselves of its value as well as of the possibility of attaining it. Therefore we have to create a mental background and a spiritual climate before we can begin with the actual practice of meditation. Without this background and the power of an inner conviction (or faith), meditation becomes a tedious exercise we have to force ourselves to do, instead of being drawn to it. This attraction is psychologically of the greatest importance, as it corresponds to the natural, and therefore spontaneous, behavior of conscious organic life.

> The behavior of an organism results from its being drawn to something, desiring something, whereas orthodox psychology, grounded in physiology and the physical sciences, is obliged to think of behavior as the result of a push or drive. (For instance, hunger, sex, fear, ambition, etc.) They are thought of as result-

ing from a chain of physical causes fundamentally like those that drive a machine. . . . It does not explain the precise directiveness of behavior. Drive will provide an organism's motive power, as it does for a car, but without something to steer it the car will have no goal, and its direction will be aimless. . . .

The difference between the contrasting concepts of "drive" and "goal," of being pushed or being drawn, seems to me much more than a quibble. It involves two unlike views of the basis of all organic activity. We are so mechanically minded that the concept of drive seems more natural to us. Actually, the idea of being drawn provides a more accurate picture of our motives as we experience them.[3]

Meditation should not be a task to which we force ourselves "with gritted teeth and clenched fists." It should rather be something that draws us, because it fills us with joy and inspiration. So long as we have to force ourselves, we are not yet ready for meditation. Instead of meditating we are violating our true nature. Instead of relaxing and letting go, we are holding on to our ego, to our will power. In this way meditation becomes a game of ambition, of personal achievement and aggrandizement. Meditation is like love: a spontaneous experience—not something that can be forced or acquired by strenuous effort. If I may be allowed to paraphrase Martin Buber's beautiful words about "true philosophy" by replacing "philosophy" by "meditation," I would formulate the quintessence of meditation in the following way: "True meditation is the meditation of a lover. He who practices such meditation, to him the hidden meaning of things is revealed, the law of things that has not yet been revealed to anybody before and which is not like something outside himself, but as if his own innermost spirit, the meaning of all his lifetime and destiny, of all his painful and exalted thought, were suddenly revealed to him."

Though the consummation of love consists in becoming one with the object of our love, this presupposes that love cannot exist without an initial object that inspires us to such an extent that we can finally identify ourselves with it. Similarly, in order to have our heart in meditation, we must be inspired by its aim and even by its initial object, because meditation is not just musing or a state of reverie, but directed consciousness or conscious awareness, which cannot exist without an object. Consciousness cannot exist without content.

To be conscious means to be aware of something. People who claim to meditate with an empty mind deceive themselves. They may be daydreaming or they may fall asleep, but that is not meditation. Consciousness is a dynamic force, in constant movement, a continuous stream. One can as little stop it as one can stop a river. Even if we could stop it, there would no longer be a river because the nature of a river consists in flowing. However, though we cannot stop a river, we can control it by diverting its flow in the desired direction. In the same way, though we cannot stop the mind we can give it direction. That means: meditation is directed consciousness.

This directedness holds true even for those who do not choose an immediate subject for their meditation because they definitely change the direction of their consciousness by turning inward. The result is a momentary or temporal sense of peace, because by turning our consciousness toward itself we slow down its flow, like a river that is dammed up and forms a quiet lake until it overflows and moves on again. This quieting down, what we may call "letting the mind rest in itself," is the first step of meditation, in which consciousness for the time being is stilled and thus remains in a state of reflection. In this state the contents of our consciousness are mirrored on its surface so that we can observe them like a spectator.

But this state alone is not sufficient, nor can we hold it for long because just as flowing water that is dammed up begins to flow over in various directions, so also our mind, unless it is channeled in a predetermined direction, begins to move here and there. By merely observing the meandering flow of our thoughts and emotions and mental images, we may get a certain insight into the functions of consciousness, but nothing more. It is here, as well as in the observation of dream states, where modem psychology stops after analyzing and interpreting the contents of consciousness thus observed. But interpretations based on an intellectual analysis of mental images and archetypal symbols are as unsatisfactory as descriptions of music in words or colors are for a blind man.

The language of words (on which our intellectual activity is based) and the language of symbols (combining visible, audible, and emotional features in which our deeper consciousness expresses itself) are two different mediums of expression and conscious awareness. The one is based on more or less fixed one-dimensional concepts with a two-dimensional logic (either-or), the other on more or less fluid multidimensional images with a correspondingly multidimensional logic. The realm of vision and the realm of thought may partly overlap, but they are never identical. The higher dimension contains the lower one, but not vice versa.

Meditation, therefore, must go beyond word-thinking, beyond thinking in concepts; it must encompass the whole human being, not only the intellect but also feeling, vision, emotional and intuitive capacity. Those who try to throw away their intellect (they are generally those who never had one) are just as mistaken as those who try to avoid all emotion (generally those who are afraid to face them). Only where heart and mind are united can genuine intuition spring up. The language of intuition, however, is that of the symbol, which presents itself as a form of inner vision because vision replaces the causal, time-conditioned relationship of the different aspects of a multidimensional object or process (which in thought can only be grasped one after another, as a succession in time) with a simultaneous awareness of all salient aspects of the envisaged symbol in accordance with the plane on which it is experienced.

Such a symbol is the figure of the Buddha, as the representative of the complete human being, a symbol that is not only visible but can be experienced in mind and body in the act of meditational and devotional practice. Those who meditate can identify themselves with the Buddha in their innermost being, even though they may still have a long way toward their final realization.

When contemplating a Buddha statue, even a person who knows nothing of the Buddha's teaching will come to the conclusion that here, indeed, is the perfect representation of the spiritualized human being who, without losing the solid ground of reality beneath his feet, accepts and ennobles his corporeality without clinging to it and without being dependent on it, and is at peace with himself and with the world. What serenity and happiness are mirrored in his face; what equanimity and tranquility in every limb of his body; what profound silence and harmony! A harmony that is contagious and penetrates the beholder! There is no more desire, no more want, no restlessness, no insecurity, no chasing after external things, no dependence on anything. There only is the highest bliss—in one word, completeness.

Those who can create and bring to life this image before their mental eye or, still more, can experience it within themselves, as the great masters of meditation did and still do, in wordless devotion and complete self-surrender: such individuals have taken the first step toward inner transformation and liberation because they have found the attitude from which the knowledge of the eternal in human beings was and ever is born.

This image of the perfected or complete human being, which has crystallized out of millennia of meditative experience, does not represent an arbitrarily isolated moment in the career of the Buddha, but the sum total, the quintessence of his spiritual activity—

something that is valid for all times and all human beings, something that is an expression of the true nature of human beings. We may not be able to define or to envisage this ultimate nature of the human being in its fullness and universality, but we can imagine and visualize to some extent a human being who embodies all the qualities that lead to the realization of this exalted state. And since our striving needs an understandable, tangible, concrete aim capable of filling us with courage and certainty, nothing can be more suitable than the figure of the Perfect Human Being, as embodied in the spiritual image of the Buddha. By transforming our own body into the living symbol of this image, by assuming the bodily posture and attitude of meditation while withdrawing the mind from all outer objects and letting it rest in its own center, we are preparing the way for the experience of final realization.

Meditation in the Buddhist sense could best be defined as "the overcoming of outer perception in favor of inner awareness," which is how Heinrich Zimmer defines "yoga." If we perceive our body in its outward material form or appearance, we are dealing with an object among other objects of the external world. We can take it to pieces, dissect it, analyze it, dissolve it into its chemical or molecular constituents, or observe its mechanism and measure the electric impulses that operate it. From this point of view, which is strictly scientific, we can completely dissociate ourselves from our body and declare our spiritual independence by denying all responsibility for our bodily existence.

But if we are inwardly aware of our body, we are no more dealing with a merely material object, a thing among other things; we are confronted with a living organism which, according to the Buddha's teaching, is the product of our mind, the basic tendencies of our consciousness, acquired through aeons of our development as conscious beings and maintained or modified through our present actions in word, deed, and thought.

In other words, our body is a form of materialized consciousness. But since this consciousness has an infinite past, it necessarily is a condensation of all universal laws and forces, focalized in the process of individualization and carried on through innumerable incarnations along the line of its inherent impetus toward an ever-increasing awareness and unfoldment of qualities, forces, or experiences accumulated in our depth consciousness.

> This gathering up of consciousness during time can be followed also through space. It stretches up through time from the placid mass of cells on the drying mud, through reptiles browsing on the branches of trees and the little mammals peeping on them through the leaves, up to Proust in his exquisite, agonizing web. So too, at this one moment of time I can feel consciousness stretching from the crystalline virus that blights tomato plants, through fish, reptiles and mammals to the minds of men. Indeed, it is obviously only an expedient convention to stop with the forms of life that are earliest in time, or the simplest in space. Consciousness must surely be traced back to the rocks that have been here since life began and so make a meeting place for the roots of life in time and space, the earliest and the simplest. Why, indeed, stop with this planet? Even if nothing like the human psyche and intellect have developed elsewhere, it is necessary in an indivisible universe to believe that the principle of consciousness must extend everywhere. Even now I imagine that I can feel all the particles of the universe nourishing my consciousness just as my consciousness informs all the particles of the universe.[4]

The fact that this consciousness is a living force and not a stagnant state, makes it clear that no permanent bodily form can represent or do justice to its nature. The very change—or better, the faculty of continual transformation—is a profound expression of the dynamic character of the mind. By looking at this change in a prejudiced, possessive frame of mind, we interpret it merely as a negative quality, instead of realizing the positive side of the process, which is not arbitrary or meaningless destruction, but a process of continual transformation according to the inherent law of the living spirit within us.

The great Sufi poet and philosopher Rumi wrote of this inherent law of continual transformation:

> I died from mineral, and plant became;
> Died from the plant, and took a sentient frame;
> Died from the beast, and donned a human dress;
> When by my dying did I e'er grow less?[5]

Those who despise the body because of its transience, therewith only prove their mental immaturity. For them the body will become a prison, while for those who recognize the body as a creation and the visible expression of the very forces that constitute our innermost being, it becomes the temple of the mind. A temple, however, by its very structure reflects the qualities and functions of its indwelling spirit. A temple that houses a universal spirit must itself represent the universe—which is exactly what the Tantras maintain. The functions of our body correspond to the functions and laws of the universe, which gradually unfold and strive to become conscious within us. The more we realize this process, the greater will be the harmony and cooperation between body and mind, the inner and the outer world, until we finally realize their essential oneness. In that moment we know that the universe itself is our true body and that we are not confined to our present physical frame in which our universal body expresses itself on the temporal three-dimensional plane.

The most obvious and the most vital function of our psychosomatic organism is the function of breathing. How vital and basic it is we can gauge from the fact that we can live without food for a number of weeks, without drink for a few days, but without air hardly for a few moments. We can relinquish even consciousness—as in deep sleep or under narcosis or in states of catalepsy—but we cannot relinquish breathing as long as we are alive. Breathing, therefore, is the most subtle function of our organism, a function that can be both conscious as well as unconscious, volitional as well as nonvolitional—in contrast to most of our other organic functions, such as the beating of our heart, the circulation of our blood, the currents of nervous energy, the functions of digestion, assimilation, and secretion, etc. Breathing is the only vital function that, in spite of its independence from our normal consciousness and its self-regulating and self-perpetuating subconscious character, can be raised into a conscious function, accessible to our mind. Due to this double nature, breathing can be made the mediator between mind and body, or the means of our conscious participation in the most vital and universal functions of our psychosomatic organism. Breathing is thus the connecting link between conscious and unconscious, gross material and fine material, volitional and automatic functions. It is the most perfect expression of the nature of all life.

The exercises leading to the deeper states of meditation therefore begin with observing and experiencing the breath, which in this way is converted from an automatic or nonvolitional function into a conscious one, and finally into a medium of spiritual forces. As such, it has been called *prāṇa* in ancient Sanskrit, a term that combines the physical as well as well as the psychic and spiritual qualities of breath—similar to our word "inspiration," which can be used in the sense of "inhalation" as well as in that of direct spiritual awareness and experience, or as the Greek word *pneuma* can signify "spirit" as well as "air."

The ancients apparently had a very profound insight into the nature of breathing and treated it not merely as a physical function but as a conveyor of cosmic energy. If, therefore, we try to impose our will upon this function without a deeper knowledge of its laws and its far-reaching effects, we are liable to cause irreparable damage to our health. On the other hand, if we try to cooperate with it consciously, without interfering with our will (our selfish intentions, our hankering after power and domination), but merely filling it with our consciousness and undivided attention (*smṛti*), then the function of breathing will not only be raised from a physical process to the level of a spiritual experience, but the whole body will be penetrated with vital energy and become conscious in its entirety, so as to be transformed into an instrument of the mind. Thus, instead of analyzing and dissecting, or merely diverting our consciousness to external movements or secondary functions of our body, we become again complete in the integration of body and mind, in which every single function derives its meaning only in relationship to the whole. The mere awareness of minor functions, isolated from their essential relations, is meaningless.

If thus we see the function of breathing against a still wider background than our momentary individual organism, then we realize that it is not only a link between the conscious and the unconscious functions of our body, but between two worlds: the inner and the outer world, the individual and the universe. For this reason the Upanishadic idea of the Atman, the universal principle in human beings, was equated with the dynamic prana, the breath of life, the vital force that streams through us, so that we partake of the Greater Life, in which the individual and the universe are one. And for the same reason the Buddha had to reverse the ancient terminology when the connotation of Atman had hardened into a stagnant, abstract concept of a changeless, immortal soul, which to the average person was indistinguishable from a glorified ego. Therefore the Buddha replaced the Atman with the *anātma-vāda*, the teaching of egolessness, which re-established the dynamic nature of life without thereby denying what is immortal in human beings. In fact, he reestablished the universality of the human being—not as an abstract principle, but as something that can be realized by overcoming the limitations of our ego illusion.

One of the most effective means for bringing about this realization is the practice of *ānāpānsati*, the contemplation and conscious experience of the process of breathing, as described in some of the most important Pali texts (like Majjhima-Nikāya and Dīgha-Nikāya). The Pali word *pāna* corresponds to the Sanskrit *prāṇa*, while *sati* is the equivalent of *smṛti* (mindfulness, remembrance, recollection) in Sanskrit. Thus *ānāpānsati* literally means "mindfulness in [the process of] inbreathing and outbreathing." The text describes in simple words, how the meditator, after retiring to a lonely place and taking the traditional cross-legged position of meditation, consciously observes the breath: "Drawing in a long breath, he knows: 'I am drawing in a long breath.' Exhaling a long breath, he knows: 'I am exhaling a long breath.' Drawing in a short breath, he knows: 'I am drawing a short breath.' Exhaling a short breath, he knows: 'I am exhaling a short breath,'" etc. It goes without saying that the meditator does not verbalize this observation, but simply is fully aware ("he knows") of each phase of the process of breathing, without mental interference, without compulsion, without violation of the natural functions of the body. Hereby not only the breathing becomes conscious, but with it also the organs through which it flows.

If the exercise was only a matter of intellectual observation and analysis of the breathing process, it would more or less come to an end at this stage. The purpose of the exercise, however, is exactly the contrary, namely, to gain a synthesis: the experience of the body as a whole, and finally the synthesis of body and mind. Our text, therefore, continues with the words, "Experiencing the whole body (*sabba-kāya*) I will inhale; experiencing the whole body I will exhale."

The next step is the stilling of all functions of the body through the conscious rhythm of the breath. From this perfect state of mental and physical equilibrium and its resulting inner harmony grows a serenity and happiness that fills the whole body with a feeling of supreme bliss, like the refreshing coolness of a spring that penetrates the entire water of a mountain lake.

Thus breathing becomes a vehicle of spiritual experience, the mediator between body and mind. It is the first step toward the transformation of the body from the state of a more or less passively and unconsciously functioning physical organ into a vehicle or tool of a perfectly developed and enlightened mind, as represented by the radiance and perfection of the Buddha's body.

The next steps are devoted to incorporating spiritual functions in the process of breathing; the object, whatever it may be, of our widening awareness, feelings, emotions, thoughts, perceptions, etc., is now associated with the functions of breathing, projected into them, experienced in them, supported by them—so that it becomes one with the universal body of the breath. It is a process that cannot be explained, but only experienced. Therefore, it can be understood only by those who have a practical knowledge of meditation, which can be gained by anyone who has the patience to proceed step by step, in which case each step will on its own accord open the way to the next higher one, in accordance with the character and the level of spiritual development of the meditator.

For this reason, all Eastern sadhanas (meditative practices) are couched in general terms, which merely serve as landmarks, leaving the individual experience untouched. While this lack of specificity may appear to be a disadvantage or a defect of the sadhana texts, in reality it is only a sensible precaution against the danger that arises from trying to imitate other peoples' experiences instead of gaining one's own. Meditation is a strictly individual affair, in spite of certain common factors of human psychology. Just as a physician cannot prescribe the same medicine to all patients, so the same sadhana cannot be given to all who want to practice meditation.

Nonetheless, certain types of practices are based on such universal principles that they can be applied to all normal human beings, like general rules for the maintenance of physical health. The practice of ānāpānsati is the most important of them, and the Buddha recommended it as the best starting point for any kind of creative meditation (*bhāvanā*). In fact, among the forty subjects of meditation mentioned in the early Pali texts, ānāpānsati is one of the few that lead to the deepest state of absorption (*appanā samādhi*).

But even the description of this sadhana can only give the framework of the meditation, which has to be filled with the meditator's own experience. Though a sunset—as a factual occurrence—is the same for all who witness it, no two people experience it in the same way. Consequently, any description of personal meditation experiences should not be regarded as a model to be imitated, but only as an example or indication of the possibilities contained in this kind of sadhana. It helps to bring about the same inspirational impetus as a poem or any other work of art created by others, which encourages us to pursue our own creative experience in a similar direction without trying to imitate anything or to hinder the spontaneity of our mind by trying to force it into a preconceived form.

Ānāpānsati distinguishes itself in this respect from *prāṇayama* (which has been popularized by many yoga teachers in the West who follow the usual Hindu tradition), in that it does not try to control (*yama*) the process of breathing, in the sense of trying to impose our will upon it—which would only assert our ego sense, the power aspect of our ego, instead of overcoming it—but tries to make us fully aware of this vital process by identifying ourselves consciously with its rhythm and its profound implications. In surrendering ourselves to its rhythm instead of interfering with it, we experience the very nature of life, for it is the rhythm of the universe that breathes through us. Instead of thinking we are the agents and originators of this movement ("I am breathing in; I am breathing out,"), we should rather feel "the universe breathes in me, streams through me; it is not I who is breathing, but the universe is breathing me."

And while experiencing this rhythm, we receive and accept the vital forces (prāṇa) of the universe with our whole being with every inhalation, and we surrender ourselves with our whole being with every exhalation. In doing so we come to realize that life consists in a continuous process of taking and giving, of receiving and relinquishing, of integration and renunciation; it is a continuous exchange and a profound interrelationship of all individual and universal forces. Whatever we receive, we have to give back; whatever we try to hold on to or to keep to ourselves will kill us. Therefore the saying, "Whosoever tries to keep his life will lose it."

We would suffocate if we tried to retain the air we have inhaled, just as we would be poisoned if we tried to keep the food we have eaten. The necessity to receive and to accept what is not ours should demonstrate to us our dependence on something greater than ourselves and make us humble, because only those who are humble have a real chance to make use of what they have received. On the other hand, to give up again what we have received should make us selfless and strengthen our capacity of renunciation. Renunciation should not be looked upon as an act of asceticism, but rather as a means of freeing ourselves of unnecessary possessions, cravings, and unworthy ambitions, by which we burden ourselves and make a prison of our existence. If renunciation is genuine, it should not be accompanied with a feeling of regret or grief, but should be a cause of joy, an act that carries in itself a feeling of deep satisfaction, like the feeling of release and satisfaction we experience in every exhalation.

Some people believe that under all circumstances renunciation is to be regarded as one of the highest qualities of the human mind, an opinion that has been favored by all more or less ascetic and otherworldly religions. But neither acceptance nor renunciation is a value in itself. Those who proudly renounce the world because they are unwilling to accept or to receive it with an open heart and mind will go the way of self-annihilation, of spiritual death, as will those who only want to receive, without giving back what they owe to the world and to their fellow beings.

Thus, the process of breathing, if fully understood and experienced in its profound significance, could teach us more than all the philosophies of the world. By raising this process into the light of consciousness, not only do we become aware of the basic functions of life, but we also have a chance to access the formative forces of the subconscious, making possible the integration of all qualities of body and mind.

The hidden formative power of Nature takes on its fullest meaning and effect for man's higher development only when he becomes conscious of its mysterious working. *Man* matures and completes himself only by becoming conscious of those great laws which, at the level of unconscious Nature, are simply lived. But this is a special form of becoming conscious. . . . It is a question not of becoming intellectually or objectively conscious of the breath life and its rhythmical order as manifested in breathing, but of becoming aware of it as a living movement in which oneself is also included, without fixing it or standing apart from it.

This *awareness* of life working within us is something fundamentally different from observing, fixing and comprehending from the outside. In such observing and comprehending he who comprehends stands apart from the comprehended and observed. But in becoming *aware*, the experience remains one with the experiencer and transforms him by taking hold of him.[6]

As long as we regard breathing as merely a physical function that consists only in filling our lungs with air and expelling it after having absorbed some of the oxygen it contains, we are far from a real understanding of what prāṇa means. The breath the ancient texts speak of is more than merely air or oxygen; it is the expression of a dynamic experience of vital force, generated with every inhalation. It does not end in reaching our lungs, but continues in our bloodstream, transforms itself into ever more subtle forms of energy conducted through the intricate system of our nerves, and thus it courses through our whole body down to the farthest extremities, until we can feel it reaching even our toes and the tips of our fingers, creating a new kind of body consciousness.

Thus, prāṇa is not only subject to constant transformation, but is able to use various mediums without interrupting its course. Just as an electric current can flow through various substances, whether solid, fluid, or gaseous, and can even flash through empty space or move in the form of radio waves if the tension or the frequency is high enough, so the current of psychic force can utilize the breath, the blood, or the nerves as conductors. At the same time it can move and act beyond these mediums by radiating from the focal points of concentrated nerve energy or centers of consciousness (chakras), if sufficiently stimulated and intensified through conscious awareness of the whole psychosomatic parallelism represented by our physical body.

This capability can be attained through the traditional posture of meditation, in which the body not only achieves its maximum centeredness, but also rests in its own center of gravity without requiring any outer support, as seen in the familiar images of Buddhas seated in the lotus position (*padmāsana*), in which a closed circuit of vital and psychic energy is created. The current flows in two interconnected circles, formed by the upper and the lower limbs, that meet in the joined hands resting upon the upturned soles of the feet in front of the solar plexus or navel center (*manipura-cakra*).

The importance of this posture—the way of sitting (asana) and the position of the hands (mudra) that characterize the attitude of meditation (dhyāna mudra)—becomes evident if we contemplate how the currents of force through the upper and lower circuits (the upper formed by chest, arms and hands, the lower by abdomen and folded legs) are joined in the hands so as to form a consecutive or infinite current in the shape of a figure 8 (which turned horizontally becomes the symbol of infinity). The fact that the hands, in which the upper and lower circuits meet, are resting in front of the vitally important navel center makes them the focal point of conscious forces. From here these forces radiate in ever-widening circles or spiral movements, until the surrounding space—which so far was only an intellectual notion—is transformed into a space filled with consciousness, into conscious space.

Since this movement extends not only horizontally, but equally upward and downward, the effect is that what until now was regarded as solid ground is felt as space—as immaterial and intangible as the air around the body. The result is a feeling of levitation, of hovering in empty space. The meditator has lost all feeling of heaviness, and even the surrounding things seem to have lost their materiality. They are perceived in a peculiar way: not singly or one after another, but simultaneously, because in place of a focal consciousness a diffused kind of awareness has emerged. It does not cling to the surfaces of things but penetrates them. Thus the process of becoming conscious of the surrounding space is at the same time a transformation of consciousness into space, a creative unfoldment of conscious space that is more than an intellectual or visual awareness of three-dimensionality. The fact that it emanates not from the head, generally regarded as the seat of consciousness, but from the navel region where the hands rest within each other, shows the importance of this center in connection with a different kind of space experience, which has its roots in a deeper region of conscious or subconscious awareness than that of our intellect. An inkling of this experience may be conveyed by the strange feeling in our solar plexus when we are confronted suddenly by empty space at the edge of a precipice.

Since our body in its embryonic state has been nourished and has grown (extended itself into space) from the navel center, we can well understand why it has been regarded as the vital and basically most important center of the human being; in China and Japan it is even thought of as the seat of the human soul. The Japanese call it *hara* and regard it as the basic center of Life (a life that is not merely an individual property, but something greater than the individual). "Just as the growth and unfolding of the crown of a tree depends directly on its root-system, so also the vital development of man's spirit depends on his being true to his roots, that is, to an uninterrupted contact with the primal unity of Life, from which human life also springs."[7]

Therefore, if meditation is to serve the development of the spirit of human beings and the completeness of their psychosomatic nature, it has to descend to the roots of life before it can rise to the heights of the spirit.

A New Way to Look at the J Ching

The deep significance of the I Ching nowadays has found recognition all over the world, even in present-day China, although Kung-Fu-tzu and the religious tenets of other great spiritual leaders and thinkers have been widely rejected. This recognition may be due to the fact that the I Ching is not based on any belief or superstition and is not bound by any kind of mythology; it represents facts of psychology and experience that embraces humanity without distinction of race or creed. In fact, it is only now, after five thousand years, that we begin to see its universal validity.

People have explored the I Ching philologically and philosophically, biologically and psychologically, metaphysically and historically, but our question is, what is the fundamental structure on which this book is based, what worldview shaped it, and what was the original conception behind it?

We find that it was expressed in the popular symbolism of its time, but we have hardly made an attempt to translate this symbolism into our modern languages. And because we are not clear about the symbolism, our understanding of the book is shrouded in mist, if not in misunderstandings.

The book may appear to most readers as a book of prophecies or oracles, as dark and mysterious as those of the Pythia of Delphi. But before it was converted into a mere oracle book, it had a clear system and structure that expressed a profound worldview. And this worldview is what interests us, irrespective of the fact that the I Ching might reveal the possibilities of our future. I say "possibilities," because this book was not written with the intention of revealing our fate or denying our free will, but rather to help us decide our way from the present into the future on the basis of generally prevailing laws. These laws are not meant to determine the future, but are indications stable enough to direct our course of action.

If we know that fire burns, we shall avoid putting our hands into it. Nevertheless, the same fire that can hurt us, can serve us in many ways if we understand its nature and respect it. So it is with all phenomena of the world; the more we respect and understand them, the easier will be the conditions of our life. Therefore, we find in the Shuo Kua: "Water and Fire complete each other."[1]

Richard Wilhelm writes in his introduction,

> After the Book of Changes [I Ching] had become firmly established as a book of divination and magic in the time of Ch'in Shih Huang Ti, the entire school of magicians (*fang shih*) of the Ch'in and Han dynasties made it their prey. . . . The task of clearing away all this rubbish was reserved for a great and wise scholar, Wang Pi, who wrote about the meaning of the Book of Changes as a book of wisdom, not as a book of divination.[2]

Though the Shuo Kua may contain elements of later times, it is primarily based on a much older tradition than the other nine Wings (as the Chinese commentaries are called), a tradition that reflects the main concept of the original worldview from which the

"Book of Transformations" (I Ching) grew. According to this tradition, "Man takes part in the forms of Heaven and Earth." "By
assimilating himself and Earth (to the universe as well as to the
conditions of his terrestrial nature) he will not get into conflict with
them." Or, as is said elsewhere in the Nine Wings: "Wisdom exalts,
morality (or ethics) makes one humble. Exaltedness imitates Heav-
en. Humility follows the example of the Earth." Here, in a few
words, the whole philosophy of life is contained.

Similarly, the eight pictures or symbols used in the eight Kuas,
though derived from nature, have a far greater implication. We can
neither take these symbols literally nor assign only one conceptual
meaning to them. We not only have to explore which meanings the
ancient Chinese attached to then, but we also have to discover how
far these meanings are applicable to the conditions of our life.

The Book of Transformations claims to depict the human situation in general, not just a particular epoch or a particular civilization. In contrast to the Bible, it does not describe the history and
the religious beliefs of a particular tribe, but is concerned with
humanity as a whole, and therein lays its importance.

The Transformations are a book, vast and great, in which
everything is contained in its completeness: the Tao of Heaven is in
it, the Tao of Earth is in it, and the Tao of Man is in it. It combines
these fundamental powers and doubles them; therefore we have six
lines that are nothing but the ways of the three fundamental powers.
"By becoming similar to Heaven and Earth, Man does not get in
conflict with them. He enjoys Heaven and knows his destiny; therefore he is free from worry. He is constant with his situation and
genuine with his sympathy. Therefore he is able to give love."[3]

The eight symbols (trigrams) on which the sixty-four hexagrams of the I Ching are based are principles that, rather than being
fixed states or conditions, are continually transforming themselves
under various circumstances. They are transitional states, which in

each case may be brought on a common denominator. We can see them from the standpoints of physiology, morphology, psychology, philosophy, metaphysics, biology, etc.

In fact, only the last five of these principles have been classified as "elements," though even they are transitional states, by which we describe certain frequently recurring conditions of our particular world of experience. Therefore, before we can make use of these symbols, we must first define them, as far as symbols can be defined. That is, we must determine on what level we want to apply them.

We cannot use one symbol in an exclusively material sense, or on the lowest level of understanding, and compare and combine it with another symbol that we take in a purely spiritual or psychological sense. When it is said, for example, "It is favorable to cross the great water," this does not necessarily mean that we have to cross the ocean, but that we have to completely change our situation, that we have to take a new step, or that we have to change our attitude thoroughly; that is, we have to begin a new life, so to say.

If someone is said to be "sown into a yellow cow-hide," it can mean the person is bound by prejudice or by common custom, while the term "yellow" stands for "earth," or the conventional usage to which we are bound. Every color in a judgment stands for a particular quality, which has neither descriptive value nor serves as a mere decoration. It refers to either certain "elements" or emotions, to certain physical or psychological qualities.

White is connected with absence of emotionality, reflective thought, intellectualism, etc.; blue with inner depth or also unfathomable emotions; and red with temperamental behavior, emotional warmth, fierce temperament, feeling more than thought, insatiable greed, or unselfish love, etc. Green may have to do with sensitiveness, but also creativeness and joie de vivre, as well as exaggerated "touchiness," etc. Yellow stands generally for an even temperament, for compromise, justice, and patience, but also indifference.

Now let us regard the Kuas from the standpoint of their linear structure or their corresponding trigrams. They appear in four groups of several degrees of polarity:

a a a	b b a	a b a	b a a
b b b	a a b	b a b	a b b
1. universal	2. organic	3. elementary	4. inorganic

I call the first group, a pair of polar opposites, "universal," because it contains the general principles of activity and passivity in their purest (unmodified) form: three strong lines and three broken lines. I call the second group "organic," because it contains the characteristics of a living organism: impulse, penetration, and assimilation, in other words, the élan vital in its creative and receptive (transforming) aspects.

The third pair is "elementary," insofar as it represents such elementary forces as fire and water, heat and cold, which can be part of the organic as well as of the inorganic. The fourth pair I have called "inorganic," because it reflects the behavior of matter, inertia and volatility: the mountain and the rising vapors (or the reflection) of the lake is a picture of peaceful, quasi-static relationship, in contrast to the other pairs of complementary opposites, especially the second, which might be called dynamic as well as organic.

Thus, the polarity that exists within each pair of trigrams repeats itself on a larger scale. The organic and inorganic group form one pair; the universal and the elementary group form another pair, as becomes clear not only through the interpretation of these signs, but also through their inherent structure. The trigrams of the universal and the elementary group are symmetrical (aaa bbb, aba bab), while the other two groups are not (bba aab, baa abb), which means that in the latter the qualitative polarity is not the only one possible.

A second kind of polarity is based on the reversed position of lines, which creates two symmetrical sides: aab–baa or bba–abb.

Thus, the hexagrams are composed of vital forces and forms that affect not only human but also all other kinds of life. They are based on the mutual relations of the two trigrams forming the hexagram and determine its meaning as well as its value, which may be creative or destructive, neutral or stagnating.

Since the I Ching is based on change, though within the limit of law, the faculty of change or transformation cannot be sufficiently stressed. All of the states of consciousness, conditions of life, states of aggregation, or other material phenomena are only transitional states, states of transformation, and as such they are moving. Thus, not only are there moving lines in certain hexagrams, but each symbol has an inherent movement, which decides its value in conjunction with other signs. Not only is whether it is moving upward or downward important, but also whether it is parallel to, supporting, compensating or confronting, diverging from or penetrating the sign it is combined with.

No sign is as such lucky or unlucky, furthering or hindering, but depends on the association with other signs, inner or outer. The momentariness of these signs makes predictions more difficult, because even if the events were fixed or foreseeable the reaction toward them is variable and depends on whether or not a person maintains the same direction in spiritual attitude or intentional behavior. Only when two movements are fixed can we predict the outcome.

The genetic code is a good example, as it shows us how apparently opposite forces, such as male and female qualities, compensate each other, cooperate with each other, and create infinite new combinations and varieties. Thus, the genetic code demonstrates convincingly and for all to see the difference between dualism and polarity, which has deceived us for centuries, since we have fallen

NEW WAY TO LOOK AT THE I CHING

into the trap of pure abstractions, fortified by logical conclusions that seem to prove the correctness of our lofty philosophical constructions and metaphysical speculations. Through them we maintain religious dogmas, even if they have no more relevance for our present times or for the real convictions of the greater part of humanity.

Our respect for past achievements or historical lifestyles often prevents us from appreciating our present reality and experience. It is true that we have been deprived of many beautiful illusions, but if we open our eyes, we will see an infinite number of things that even the most romantic imagination of the past could not conceive —even such things as obvious to us as the beauty of landscapes, like those of the Alps, the Himalayas, or the Andes, which only a few centuries ago were regarded with undisguised horror.

And though the moon, which inspired past generations with poetry and lofty feelings, may for the present generation be a heap of dust and ashes, a dead body, circling our earth, nonetheless what may disappoint us because it does not verify our former beliefs may still fill us with wonder, if we free ourselves from former prejudices.

One of our greatest prejudices consists in seeing ourselves in contrast to the world that surrounds us, leading to our desire either to escape from it or govern it. Both cases are consequences of an ingrained dualism, which splits the world into self and non-self. But nature, as we have seen not only in the genetic code, but also in all other laws of life, which already have compelled us to reverse our attitude to our surroundings, is not based on dualism but on polarity.

The difference between dualism and polarity consists, as we cannot repeat often enough, in the fact that dualism is only capable of seeing incompatible opposites, which leads to one-sided evaluations and decisions and cuts the world into irreconcilable contrasting parts, while polarity is born from unity and includes the concept of the completeness of an organic whole. The respective poles complement each other and are inseparably bound to each other, like the positive and the negative poles of a magnet, which condition each other and can never be separated. The mistake of dualism consists in trying to accept only one side of life, namely that which corresponds to our wishes or ideals, or which favors our clinging to our present condition, our illusory self and all that identifies itself with it.

Thus, the concept of changeless is identified with duration or continuity. But according to the Book of Transformations, "Duration is a condition whose movement is not exhausted by hindrances. It is not a state of rest [in the sense of motionlessness], because a mere standstill is regression. Duration, therefore, is a self-renewing movement of an organized and integrated whole, which proceeds in conformity with unalterable laws."[4] In this sentence, the central idea of the I Ching has been brought into its shortest formulation, which even modern science can accept.

But again we have to point out that law is not determinism, but a regulative principle without which freedom of any kind would not be possible. Just as we cannot walk on ice without friction, resistance is necessary for our progress, physically as well as spiritually.

In spiritual life, we cannot rely exclusively on our intuition; we need to give it a structure, be it in the form of symbols, logic, or mathematics. This structure is nothing final, and when it has served its purpose we may abandon it. But those who abandon it before that time are dreamers who lose themselves in their dream. If we want to awaken to the reality of our own life or experience, we have to use both reason and imagination.

Chapter 7

Questions and Answers
Human Dimensions Seminar,
June 1975

Lama Govinda: I am turning it over to all of you to set the theme because today we are having a darshan, which means that we are just in each other's presence. I am not giving a lecture, but you are free to put any subject before us, any question, or any problem, and we will discuss what you are interested in. Without knowing you and your own interests, I will not know what is best to discuss, so please let us regard this as a kind of a two-way discussion and mutual understanding. I think that is much better than just to talk on some abstract subject. So please let me hear what you would like to talk about.

Question: I would like to ask about mantras. I would like to know if there will ever be any American mantras, or if chanting must always be done in Sanskrit or in the Japanese language?

Lama Govinda: I think that is a very good question. It is a question that is rather important to consider, because I find since we came back to America that so many people are talking about mantras and chanting mantras. Yet so far I have not found people who really know what the mantra means, and I know that there are some who will simply give a mantra and leave people with it, saying, "Now you make out of it what you like." Well, that is a misunderstanding, a very profound misunderstanding, because, first of all, a mantra is not a meaningless thing. Second, there are different kinds of mantras; there are archetypal major mantras and archetypal word symbols.

In order to understand any of that, we have to know the meaning of the word "mantra"; it means an instrument or tool of the mind. Now, before we can use a tool we have to know how to use it. If somebody placed an unfamiliar tool in your hand you wouldn't know what to do with it. So, as with any tool, we have to know first how to use it.

Secondly, in India the mantra has never been used in any other way than as a kind of final seal of initiation. Therefore, the mantra is the end, the end point of certain spiritual development. It is not the beginning, but a part of the end, a point of initiation, and then a new thing begins. Actually, there is no final end in that respect, but it is the end of training—the end of the preparation for the actual work. So a mantra without initiation is not a mantra but just a plaything or something that might help you to relax; but a mantra is more than just a means for relaxation. The idea is that before initiation can take place there must be training and certain knowledge. Only after that stage has been developed, at the end of the preparation, does the mantra confirm, like a seal, whatever has been experienced or absorbed.

There is a difference between a bīja mantra, which means a seed mantra, and a more composite mantra, which contains certain symbols. In both cases, we are dealing with archetypal symbols but the bīja mantra is not only archetypal, but also a prelingual sound. It is not a fixed sound, which is a concept or a word. Before language existed certain sounds conveyed certain meanings. Before a child can speak, it will utter simple vowel sounds. So the vowel is the foundation of language. The Indian alphabet doesn't start *a b c d e*, etc.; instead, it begins with all vowels. First come the vowels, then the consonants. Again, the vowels are based on the first of the vowels, *a* (AH). "AH" is the basic sound of all language. Therefore the bīja mantra *a* (AH) stands for language, for culture, for human knowledge—because everything we call human knowledge is based on language. We cannot think without language. We cannot understand things. Language is the particular human capacity to interpret the world in which we live.

The original sounds are vowel sounds; then we have sounds you can call the low sounds or high sounds. Every sound has a certain vibration. Here I mean vibration as in a musical or physical sense: the quicker vibration is understood as a sound that is upward moving or high. We automatically speak of high notes or low notes without actually knowing why we do so, but if we examine them from a different point of view we will see that the low sounds have longer vibrations and the high sounds have quicker vibrations. Once we establish the direction of low or high, then we can also see an in-between, with the middle sounds. So you could say, for instance that E, high E, is going up and that U (OO) is going down and *a* (AH) would be in the middle. That means you have horizontal sound and vertical sounds.

These ideas are basic. But the vowels alone do not yet make a mantra, as you can see when you look at Sanskrit. There you will see that all the mantric sounds have a little circle, or a little dot, on top of the vowels and this little ring means actually that we close off the sound. It means that the sound is closed off either in the throat or in the sense of a nasal sound. And what happens? The sound is first emitted outward, then closed off so that it turns inward, going from the audible into the inaudible. The second part, the inaudible vibration, is actually not a sound vibration as we hear it with our ears, but a psychic vibration that awakens certain centers of our consciousness. This is the basic idea of the bīja mantra.

Now, the secondary form is that we regard certain words, for instance, as symbol words, and again these symbols must be archetypal symbols. I distinguish these from ordinary symbols, artificially made symbols like those you find everywhere in commerce and in technology (and every year you have all sorts of abbreviations, which are used to mean this or that, or even signs like perhaps a winged wheel for the railway). They are arbitrary symbols designed for a particular purpose, which only have meaning within a certain group or a certain country. Archetypal symbols are symbols that are connected with the structure of our consciousness; therefore they are more universal than the ordinary word. They convey a meaning that, so to speak, belongs to the deeper regions of our consciousness. For instance, in India a word like *padma*, which means the lotus, has many different meanings. It not only means the flower lotus, but is also a synonym for *chakra*. It means anything that unfolds; it means unfoldment of a spiritual quality or the center of radiation, that is, the center of consciousness. At the same time, it means the symbol of purity. The symbols of so many things have gone into these words because they have been used through thousands of years. When such words are connected with the bīja mantras, they again get a particular and more definite meaning.

Now, to give you a definite example, one of the basic mantras, or bīja mantras, especially in the Buddhist tradition, is OṀ -A- HŪM. Notice that the Oṁ has the roundness and all-inclusiveness that is also expressed in the Greek letter Omega and in the Roman lettering around the circle, so I think it is not arbitrary—it really is because those who created script had the feeling of this particular movement, this kind of circular movement. So in the Oṁ you get this kind of opening and widening, inclusiveness. When you come

to the A (AAAAHHHHH), you are in the middle, and then with
HŪM you go down.

Now, these three sounds are connected with the three centers of
consciousness. The crown, the *sahasrāra* chakra, the highest chakra,
is not entirely identified with the brain, but nevertheless the brain is
certainly connected physiologically, I would say, with it. But the
OM, as you see from this, is a universal sound and therefore the
foremost sound used before any other mantra. Particularly in Buddhism, you will never find the Om at the end. You will find it there
in some mantras in Hinduism, where things have perhaps not been
so much systematized, or at least because there are so many Hindu
traditions that mantras are used more in a devotional way. In Buddhism a mantra is not just devotional—it really is connected with a
particular chakra or with particular centers of consciousness.

So the Om is the universal sound; it stands first. A (AH), which
is in the middle, refers to the center for human speech and thought.
In fact, our whole human, particularly human, type of consciousness is only possible, as I said before, through language, which has
to do with our particular thoughts, the possibility of thought. The
HŪM is related to the heart center, and again here I want to make
it clear that this has nothing to do directly with the heart as the
pumping station of the blood. It means the center, which is here in
the middle and is the emotional center: emotional in the very deep
sense. So if you use OM-A-HŪM it means that the universal experience has to go down, has to be realized in the human center, in our
deepest emotional center—it has to be reborn in our heart. If you
would live only in universal conception, you would live in a world
that wouldn't touch the human world. It would be something
beyond, and though it might contain all that is human, it would not
allow us to reach that particular application in our present human
state. Therefore, the universality of the OM has to be realized in the
heart center, which is expressed through the mantra HŪM.

The next question is, "How do we get a composite mantra?" I will just give you this one example, like the OṀ MAṆI PADME. The middle word between the OṀ and the HŪM, which was represented above by A (AH) has been expressed by two archetypal symbols. One is PADMA, in this case, PADME, the other is MAṆI, which means "jewel." Here again, as also I think in most other languages, "jewel" is a symbol that has more to it than the actual precious stone. It means anything that is precious. "Jewel" expresses the preciousness, and in this case it means what is most precious for a human being—what you can imagine is for you divine. In our case we would speak of the Buddha as the embodiment of all the divine qualities of a human being and the PADMA as being the lotus of our own heart. That means we have to realize the ideal of Buddhahood, of divine wisdom and realization, within our own heart.

My book *Foundations of Tibetan Mysticism* originally had the title "OṀ MAṆI PADME HŪM," but I found that somebody else had written a book with that very title. The book was about an expedition to a monastery, and that title was used just as a symbol of something Buddhist, but without going into it. Because of that, I had to find another title for my book, so I called it "Foundations of Tibetan Mysticism"—because in this one mantra, which took me a whole book to explain, I actually give an indication of what can be the seed of all mantras. It was a good example. And now you will find, for instance, that in most Hindu mantras you will certainly hear the OṀ. It is basic for both Buddhism and Hinduism; it is a universal symbol, as I say, and is rightly used by both religions. Perhaps it may also have something to do with "Amen" in Christianity, though I think "Amen" is perhaps more a confirmation of intentions. I don't know what it means in Hebrew, but I think that is the way it is used, because if it is used at the end of the prayer, it certainly has to do with a kind of confirmation and surrender.

Anyway, you must have heard many of the Hindu groups nowadays chanting Hindu mantras: "Om Hari Krishna Om," and so on. In this case, "Hari" stands for Vishnu and "Krishna" stands for an incarnation of Vishnu, for the avatar of Vishnu. In this case, the two words in the middle are the different names of the particular divine conception of Hinduism. So here, the people, while chanting this mantra, feel themselves in the presence of their particular aspect of God. I say "aspect of God" because in India each divine quality has been embodied in a particular form. We speak of Brahma, Vishnu, and Shiva. Now in the higher philosophy, Advaita philosophy, you understand that these are aspects of the divine and that the ultimate divine actually cannot be described or explained, so you speak of the neutral Brahman, which has no designation anymore—you can call it everything, or you can call it the unspeakable, or the unexplainable. In Buddhism, we perhaps have a parallel to this, but a parallel of a slightly different attitude, when one speaks, for instance, about śūnyatā.

Question: Would you please discuss attachment?

Lama Govinda: Attachment! People generally, Buddhists especially, use the word "attachment" in a very negative sense, and yet I don't feel guilty if I feel attached to friends or to so many people whom one loves. As always happens, we use words, and the moment we use them we are caught in a trap. Hardly any word has only one meaning, and if we really want to know what "attachment" is, we have to ask not only about the word, but also about what you are attached to. Attachment has to be qualified. Attachment can be bad and can be good. If you are attached to bad things, well, that's bad.

And if you are attached to good things or to good feelings and to good qualities, that is quite a different thing.

We will see that if one is attached to the Dharma, to the great universal reality in the sense of the universal law of religion or the highest things we can think of, that is not a bad attachment. But if, on the other hand, the attachment is to a concept of the Dharma, to a particular formulation of the Dharma, then it becomes a really different thing and may result in intolerance or in limitations.

In Buddhism, there is a difference between *karma chanda* and *Dharma chanda*. Karma chanda means to be attached to sensual objects and/or to sensual love, and Dharma chanda means to be attached to the highest aspirations. So both are attachments. And again, the Buddha, who knew the danger that people could misunderstand even Dharma chanda, said that the Dharma in the form of a formulation, in the form of a teaching, even his own teaching, is like a raft. The raft is meant to cross the river, but once you are on the other shore you don't carry the raft about on your head. You leave it, and you are free from it. In the same way, his influence is like a raft. It will carry you over the stream, but don't get attached to it. I think this attitude is the most beautiful and most liberal that our religious leaders ever have had. I am again and again reminded of it.

Another point is that people may say, well, the more you are attached, in the sense that you love others, the more you will suffer. Here I have to ask, "Is suffering perhaps a small price for the privilege of having love, of having others?" I would rather take upon myself the suffering of loving others, than to have no love at all. The kind of saintliness, if it is really saintliness, of people who have come to that state of so-called perfection and are untouched by anything happening around them leaves me cold, and I would not wish for that.

I also think that many people who are perhaps in a kind of despair because they think, "How can I ever get free? I have so many attachments, I have this and that, and so on," should only ask themselves what they mean by attachment. If they are attached to money, if they are attached to goods, if they attached to things, to places, to all these different objects of possession, then attachment creates a prison, creates bondage.

So we have to distinguish between attachment that becomes possessiveness and attachment that is the inner bond between beings who love each other or care for each other or even have compassion for each other. Love between a husband and a wife, between a mother and a child, between friends, and so on, an attachment that is very loving. But we have to guard against wanting. Even the love of a mother for her children can become an expression of possessiveness. And the moment attachment becomes possessive it becomes negative.

Here is an interesting story: It is said that when the Buddha passed into nirvana all the Arhats sat around entirely aloof, and only one, Ananda, who was deeply attached, burst into tears. And the great saints blamed Ananda afterward and said, "You have not yet attained the highest and you must be excluded from the conference." [The conference referred to took place to establish the Dharma.] This story shows how people always get a strange idea that complete detachment is equal to saintliness. To my mind Ananda was probably the only one who had deeply understood, and he was the one who later on was able to recite practically all the sacred texts, because he had been the constant companion of the Buddha.

In the scriptures, though he is often shown still asking questions of all kinds, he seems to be the most lively of all the people, and I think that was the difference. Most people thought the main message of the Buddha was the words he spoke, while Ananda knew that the Buddha's presence was more than the words. And

121

that is true about the presence of the Buddha. Even after he had bodily passed away, he remained spiritually with all of them. Ananda was certainly more human, and I prefer one tear of Ananda to all the other Arhats, who were very accomplished.

Question: Should we meditate upon universal love?

Lama Govinda: Now, this question also applies to the question of meditation. Meditation should not be something removed from life, removed from our feelings and inner attachments. When we try to generate love and compassion for all living beings in our meditation, I think it is much more to the point to think of our direct relationships with the beings around us. If people speak of universal love, I am afraid they are having a beautiful concept, but love is really a relationship, an individual relationship.

We can have compassion, which is quite different. We can have compassion without even perhaps having a direct relationship, a personal relationship, with others, and I think we can also have pure friendliness, from the start, toward everybody. One can feel that, and one can feel sympathy. That is one thing. But I will say that this kind of sympathy would be a kind of openness, while love always means a direct relationship between human beings. And so, therefore, I think, it is much more honest, if we want to dwell on the feelings of love, to dwell on the very people around us and examine how far we are capable of extending our love to them.

Certain people find loving difficult, while other people do love. You may find as you meditate that you prefer to love some people, because they agree with you or are giving you advantages. And then there are those who perhaps are very different beings or perhaps are obstacles in your life, people you don't love or perhaps even hate. So I think it is much more fruitful, even in this type of meditation, to realize, to put before our mental eye, the direct relationship with the people we come in touch with, before we go into purely abstract ideas of universality and so on.

Question: Should we think about something when we meditate?

Lama Govinda: Well, one kind of preparatory thing is preparatory thoughts, because, after all, in the beginning meditation has to do also with our thinking. Our mind goes on thinking always, at least as long as we are conscious—the activity doesn't stop. Even if you want to stop and try to force ourselves to, it won't stop; we find that the process is still going on.

So the only way to control that process is either to observe how it halts or proceeds, or to follow that flow of thought in seeking where it leads. Or there's a second possibility: to have some clear object in our mind as the subject of our contemplation or meditation.

But what is more important is that we *become*. There's no end to all these processes. And finally we come to a deeper point. That is, we suddenly begin to feel conscious of consciousness. And you have the very feeling that you are here and now, and that is actually the greatest miracle—that you have become conscious of being here. If, when you come to that level, you suddenly find there's something much deeper than our thoughts, then an opening begins, and this opening is the beginning of real meditation.

Some days ago, I had a group who asked, what is meditation— in a few lines? I will repeat the answer here, because I found that many of those present asked about it and thought it a useful definition. So let me put it into this short form: Meditation is the means to reconnect the individual with the whole, that is, to make the individual conscious of the connection. It is the only positive way to overcome the ego complex, the illusion of separateness, which no amount of pious preaching and exhortation will achieve. To give up

123

the smaller for the bigger is not a sacrifice, but a joyous release from oppression and narrowness. The selfishness resulting from this experience is not due to lower considerations of pleasures, but is a natural attitude free from the feeling of moral superiority. The compassion that flows from this attitude is the natural expression of the solidarity of all life. Meditation, however, is the means not only to realize our connection with the whole, but also to become conscious that every individual is a unique opportunity to become a focal point in which the universe becomes conscious of itself.

Question: What do you mean by concentration?

Lama Govinda: The focalization of our consciousness is what we generally call concentration. But there are different kinds of concentration. To be focalized in our concentration does not mean necessarily to be focalized on one particular idea or one particular content. We have ways; we know that when we are doing some work, we are concentrated on the work—and we also know that if we want to solve a problem, we concentrate on the different parts and expressions of that problem.

But there is also a different kind of concentration, and that is rather a centering around some idea or some direction. It means, in other words, you can establish a direction within yourself without confining yourself to one point only, and here, I would say, East and West have different ideas about what concentration is. The Western mind has the attitude of going straight in one line toward one object, one idea, to the exclusion of everything else. In one way, that's good, but in another way, it is a great limitation, because if we really want to explore something, we should go around the subject of our exploration rather than trying to see the object of our investigation from only one perspective. So this kind of a concentric approach to things is different from the arrow-like direction,

and the Eastern way is much more in the way of concentric movement around it.

These differing approaches also make clear why there is a sincere difference between Eastern and Western art. In Western art, at
least until recently, the principle of perspective held that we should
view every object only from one side, but Eastern art, in general,
and particularly its more ancient form (also, by the way, the art of
the European Middle Ages), took a different way. Perspective doesn't
play an important role, and often there is no perspective at all.

Now most people mistake meditation for the simple act of concentration. That this is not so is evident, because the bookkeeper
bent on his figures and calculations is also concentrating intently,
but he is not meditating. Very often our great wish to concentrate
can become a hindrance, namely if it becomes a compulsion.

So sometimes in the beginning I will say it is very good just to
observe our flow of thought before we settle down, before we come
to the planes of our own being. Instead of opposing that movement within us, it becomes better to flow with it, and if we do it
brings us to the state of tranquility in which we can then find our
inner direction.

I just said that meditation is not only a means to realize our
connection with the whole, but also a way to become conscious of
every individual as a unique opportunity to become a focal point in
which the universe becomes conscious of itself. I want to go into
this here. The process involves not only the experience of universality, but also the experience of the uniqueness of the individuality
that makes this experience possible and fills us with a sense of
responsibility toward the very vehicle or instrument of this experience in which the universe manifests itself.

True meditation does not lead to the extreme of self-annihilation
or dissolving into the featureless All, nor does it lead into a state
of indifference toward the world in which we live or the body and

its senses through which we experience this world. On the contrary, it enables us to see it in a greater frame, in a bigger connection that transforms the trivialities of our mundane life into deeply significant aspects of a cosmic play in which we are both the actors and the spectators.

Question: What is meant by "cosmic play"?

Lama Govinda: When we speak of a "cosmic play," most people mistake play for waywardness. They think play is just something in which we can let ourselves loose, but if we think a little more about it, can there be any play, or even any ordinary game, without some rules? Even in an ordinary football game, you have to follow some rules.

We are quite free to move about and to act on our own individuality, so if we find we can play the game, we have to know the rules of the game. And the rules of the game, in the universal sense, are synonymous with what you call Dharma, so without understanding the Dharma, we cannot exert our freedom in the play in which we take part. Also, if we think of a theater play, for example, everyone must know his or her role, which can only be understood in relationship to the whole play. In the same sense, we can understand our position in life, and our position in the world in which we live.

So one of the lessons or reasons for meditation is to become certain of our role in life, our own position, and our responsibilities—because there can be no freedom without responsibility. Freedom is not just doing what we like; freedom is doing what is right in our position and what conforms to the rules of the greater play in which we take part.

The East has a term, *līlā*, that means something like "universal play." I do not think the term has any real correspondence in Western terminology. We all have heard the idea of karma. Now, līlā and karma are related, like freedom and necessity, like law and spontaneity. They are not exclusive because if there were not certain laws, you couldn't even live—that table, or any other material thing, has a weight and remains where it is according to the law of gravitation. Now if the law of gravitation did not exist, everything would be flying about, everything would go into the universe. And so it is actually the limitations of laws that make it possible for us to be free and to make our own decisions within the framework of that law.

A musician who wants to create music has first to know the laws of harmony and to know an instrument and to practice, and so on. And only after the inner laws of music have been understood do these very same laws give the freedom to express exactly what the individual feels. So individual expression is not a contradiction to the universal or particular law of the world in which we live.

In that sense, the highest art is līlā. It overflows from the artist like a song from a bird. It is not for the sake of gain, reward, or acclaim but is the free, spontaneous expression of an overwhelming inner experience. The greatest artists, however, are those who convert their whole life into a work of art, and that, in turn, into the perfect sage.

We cannot believe in freedom without believing in līlā. Without freedom, there can be neither morality nor virtue. Now, I spoke of līlā and karma, freedom and necessity. The question here is, how does līlā fit into the law of karma? We can say that karma is the necessary outflow of an ego-related action; that means as long as our action is egocentric, related only to our self or to our imaginary ego, we are bound to that very action; it remains, so to speak, centrifugal the whole time and comes back to us.

But a spontaneous action is līlā, that is, an action that is not premeditated in order to have an advantage or to gain something for our own person. It is something that flows freely from us. It is free from karma, and therefore it defeats karma. Generally, karma means simply action, and usually when we use the word "karma," we really mean an action that creates reaction. So, correctly speaking, karma means the action of our deeds. Therefore, the deliberate action we are generally accustomed to turns finally into spontaneous action, and the moment it becomes spontaneous, it becomes free.

In the same way, concentration can become finally—from the intentional concentration upon one point or one idea—the concentration of being simply centered within us. In that moment, our concentration becomes spontaneous, and then it leads to inner unification, which is the aim of meditation.

So, karma-free, purpose-free, unselfish action is possible only if we perform our way in life as good actors perform their roles, forgetting the private personality. Actors who think and live in the reality of what they are and what they should be as an actor will be a bad actor. In the same way, the whole perfection in līlā is to play our role in complete forgetfulness of our egohood, of our separation; that means we must always play it in relationship to everything around us. That is what Buddhahood actually stands for.

Buddhism says that we are interrelated with everything that exists. The whole world is like a tremendous net of relationships. There is not one thing that is not related to all the other things in the universe. And for that reason we can say that every individual is a crystallization of all that is contained in the universe. All the forces of the universe are necessary to create even one human being or even one tree or even one insect. Without the basis of the entire forces of the cosmos, not a single individual could come into appearance. And if we look at it this way, we begin to wonder whether it is not perhaps the highest achievement of this universe to become individualized in various forms of life.

If we see the universe as a whole and realize the vast emptiness and the very rare occurrences of the crystallization of forms of what we call matter, which made living and conscious beings possible, then perhaps we will be able to understand that individuality is as important as universality. In fact, universality can only be experienced through individuality. Let me say again that it was perhaps necessary for the universe to create individuals in order to become conscious of itself.

Question: I thought we were supposed to overcome our individuality, our ego?

Lama Govinda: To become individualized does not mean that one has to become egocentric. That is, again, one of the many misconceptions people have—to think that in order to overcome our egoness, we must simply deny our individuality. It is due to our wrong conception of our psyche, of our psychological ideas.

I would suggest a very simple way to depict our consciousness: Imagine a circle. You have a periphery and a center. Our concentration, as we see it, is actually upon the relationship of the periphery to the center. The center is the point in which all concentration becomes one. The periphery is the part in which concentration is individualized. If we live only entirely on the periphery, then we are separated from the center and we become limited—and not only limited, for we also become cut off from the source of life. On the other hand, if you were to live only in the center, you would deny individuality and you would be unconscious of all universality.

So it seems to me, that in meditation, we have to establish the relationship between the periphery and the center, and the highest achievement we can have is to find a middle distance between periphery and center, in which we can partake of both. That means a middle place in which our individuality becomes a reflection of our universal center. In this form, we become complete and realize the abundance of our faculties.

The ego function is in no way essential to the individual, to the total human organism in fulfilling and expressing its individuality, for every individual is a unique manifestation of the whole, as every branch is a particular outreaching of the tree. To manifest individually, every branch must have a sensitive connection with the tree, just as our independently moving and differentiated fingers must have a sensitive connection with the whole body. The point, which can hardly be repeated too often, is that differentiation is not separation. The head and the feet are different, but not separate. And though human beings are not connected to the universe by exactly the same physical relations as branch to tree, or feet to head, they are nonetheless connected, and by physical relations of fascinating complexity.

Question: What about death and reincarnation?

Lama Govinda: The death of the individual is not disconnection, but withdrawal. The corpse is like a footprint or an echo, a dissolving trace of something that the self has ceased to do. In another connection, we say we are not born into the world, but out of the world. This statement is true, because the eternity of the world is at the base of our existence, so the universe is ultimately our own created body.

This idea of the universe as our greater body has been represented in Buddhist terminology as the Dharmakāya. It is said that every enlightened one exists in three bodies, and to a certain extent, even we exist in three bodies—the Dharmakāya, the Sambhogakāya, and the Nirmāṇakāya, which mean the universal body in which we all share, the body of spiritual enjoyment, and the body of transformation.

The body of transformation is actually what we call our material body in which our consciousness has been crystallized. According to Buddhist psychology, we are not different from our body, and we are not, so to say, taking a body, as in the idea of transmigration according to relative ideas—that the soul suddenly goes into a ready-made body or goes from one body to another. That conception has been greatly misunderstood. In Buddhism, there is no such idea.

The idea of rebirth in Buddhism is that the consciousness itself crystallizes and forms the body from the very first point of conception. So we actually regard our body now as the crystallization of our past consciousness, and that is why we feel sometimes a difference between our present body and what we are now in our mind. Our body feels as if it is lagging behind, because it represents the previous state of our consciousness, while our consciousness has probably already gone ahead; then we find the discrepancy between our body and mind. But in reality there is no such discrepancy. It is only that we represent two different time moments or time sections in the form of the material crystallization and in the form of our already flowing consciousness.

Our body moves in a continuous state of flux. We know that even in seven years not one particle of our body will remain the same. Every particle within our body will be replaced within seven years, and yet the great wonder is that although not a single particle remains the same, the bodily form has continuity. This continuity means there is a central forming principle within us, which reestablishes or keeps the direction of our form and ensures that though there is a change, the change is not an abrupt change, but a slow transformation.

Thus we can say that though the body of the child is not the same as the body of a grown-up person, there is a transition from the child's body to the body of a grown-up person. And the continuity we observe here in the body is the same continuity that goes on in our mind. There are not two seconds in which our consciousness is the same. So the flux is quicker with changes in the consciousness than with changes in the body, but in both cases, it is flux.

If we want to come to terms with our body in meditation, we see that in a certain way the universe reflects within ourselves, insofar as we now try to become conscious of the totality of our body. In that way, we can recondition our body according to the state of our plane of consciousness. This process can only happen if we really go into a deep state of meditation in which the body is not excluded. That is one of the reasons we need special asanas, which are ways we sit in meditation.

In order for the body to respond to our meditational experience, we have to establish a deeper connection between body and mind, and the best connection is our breathing. Breathing is the mediating function, because it can be both automatic and volitional. You can't dictate the beating of your heart, you can't control the functions of digestion, you can't control the bloodstream, and so on. All those things are automatic qualities, and generally your breathing also has become an automatic faculty. But the breathing is subtler than all the other faculties and therefore nearest to our mind, and it can, if it shows its relationship to our consciousness, become a volitional or experienceable quality.

So breathing is what connects body and mind, and if you understand breathing as an experience, not just as a habit—if you become conscious of your breathing function and follow it through your body—then you can feel it as it flows through the totality of your body. In the way it does so, finally, you will feel that your consciousness fills the whole body, and in that moment your body partakes of your meditational experience.

Question: What is the relationship between nirvana and samadhi?

Lama Govinda: Samadhi is a state of inner unification; nirvana is a more permanent state, meaning the overcoming of greed, hatred, and ignorance. While in samadhi, you have a momentary state of complete unification, but it is not necessarily permanent. So nirvana is a different concept. Also, there is a difference between the concept of nirvana in Hinduism and in Buddhism.

In Hinduism, nirvana is more or less a metaphysical concept. In Buddhism, it is a purely psychological concept, which can be defined as the overcoming of greed, hatred and ignorance. And in this case, greed and hatred mean that the attraction and rejection are really two extremes in our attitude toward things. Ignorance means the misconception of having an entirely separate being, or ego, from others. So in Nirvana, you have completely overcome these hindrances.

Question: What is the singing we sometimes hear in our ears when we are in meditation in a group?

Lama Govinda: Well, that is what we call *shata*. Shata is a sound. When you are very still, you can hear many different sounds. According to the old scriptures, you can hear the sound of thunder, the sound of a flute, the sound of a bird, etc. All of these sounds are different, and there is a special type of meditation, *shata nova*, in which you assist inner sounds as part of concentration. Instead of concentrating upon an object with your eyes, you can have a flame before you, you can have a picture before you, you can have nature, you can look out at the space—all of these are means of concentration. Instead of an individual point of concentration, you can also concentrate on that inner sound, and it is said that there are different sounds that should show you different levels of consciousness.

For instance, the sound of bells is a well-known sound that comes and sharpens the state of consciousness. And it can become so intense that after some time you may not even be conscious whether it is inside or outside. So suddenly you may hear beautiful bells, and then you realize that nobody else hears them. Only you.

Question: You mentioned that līlā being spontaneous action, complete in itself, doesn't leave any karma. Could you please elaborate on that? If every action creates karma ...

Lama Govinda: No, not every action. You see, the definition of karma is volitional action. For instance, if you had no intention, if the action is just spontaneous action, which is not intended action, not a thought-out action, and not an action related to your ego sense, then it is karma free. But the moment it is related to your ego sense and initiated by your ego, it reflects to your consciousness.

Question: How does anger fit into that?

Lama Govinda: If you are angry because, for instance, somebody has hurt you or insulted you, then this anger certainly creates karma. Because you will continue to get angry at whatever happens that is similar. You will get angry again, that anger will occur again. The more often it occurs, the more you get into that trend of getting angry. On the other hand, if you refrain or think to yourself "Well, why should I get angry, nobody can be changed by it," and you quiet down, in then you will have established a precedent that later on will help you in similar situations.

Question: Well, isn't that karma, though—stopping the anger rather than the spontaneous thing that came without intention?

Lama Govinda: Yes, anger may be quite spontaneous, but it is spontaneously ego-centered. The point is not just spontaneity, but also ego-centeredness and ego-relatedness. It is quite true that in spontaneous action one has to distinguish between purely intuitively spontaneous action and the spontaneous action triggered by our ego sense.

Question: Is it good to let anger come out?

Lama Govinda: Sometimes, it is good, yes. Some people may repress anger; at least they are angry, but they don't change, because they repress it. They don't let it out, so the anger remains with them. There is no outlet, and it may sometimes be injurious. On the other hand, if you give it too much free expression, it will carry you further than you will actually want to go. So, I think, it all depends on the situation. In certain cases it is better to express it in a free way, so long as we do not hurt others by it.

Question: A child will bang a table …

Lama Govinda: Well, that is a good outlet, if the table isn't smashed.

Question: If we are so connected to the universe, why are we told to experience nothingness, or emptiness— śūnyatā?

Lama Govinda: Most people get frightened when they hear about śūnyatā because it has been considered as emptiness. Now we can't experience emptiness unless we know what is the opposite of emptiness. In the beginning emptiness seems to be a very negative expression, yet if we are in meditation or in prayer and want to receive anything, we first have to be empty. Unless the vessel is empty, it can't receive. So emptiness in this case becomes a very positive quality because it gives space for something to be received.

But it is meaning, and if we look at the universe as we know it nowadays in modern physics, we notice to our astonishment and perhaps even to our horror that this whole huge universe is mainly emptiness and that actually matter is the rarest creation in this universe. If we think about it, we begin to wonder if we have not misunderstood what matter is and if our whole conception of materialism is a misnomer—because we have not yet reached the state of real materialism. To be real materialists means to be people who understand the meaning and importance of matter.

Then I can think it would be almost synonymous with spiritualism because matter means only a concentration of energy in a balanced state, so that it can keep or take certain forms. That state, it seems to me, is probably the highest achievement of the universe. Without matter there would be no possibility of living beings, or consciousness. In other words, matter is the basis on which the universe can become conscious of itself in its living individuals.

So I think we should have a deep respect for matter and should handle it accordingly and not misuse it. We should be like St. Francis of Assisi, who spoke of Sister Water and Brother Fire, Sister Moon and Brother Sun. He immediately understood and experienced all of the different elements as living qualities and divine presences.

What really went on before religions were institutionalized was a great reverence for the earth, for the water, for the fire and the air and the wind and the sun, and all of it. You can see it among the American Indians. Nowadays we think this reverence is primitive, but I think these people had a much more refined feeling for the world in which they lived than we do now.

We have objectified everything, and that's why we are objecting to everything—I think that is extremely profound, and sometimes language itself shows us, as if in a mirror, our own misconceptions.

Question: In regard to an emotion like anger, how can you discriminate between quieting down and repressing it?

Lama Govinda: Well, the moment you begin to think and try to find out why you are angry, most of your anger is gone, because you have disengaged your consciousness from the limitation that caused the anger. Some people say that before you get angry, count up to thirty or something like that. You do that and by the time you have counted to thirty, you have forgotten what you were angry about. So it is always a good thing to give pause and to understand.

Question: Before it can take hold?

Lama Govinda: Yes, before it can take hold of you. Many people get in a kind of unreasonable anger or they start at a point that was perhaps quite genuine and simply let themselves go, and it carries them much further than they ever intended; there was no justification for that. So it is always good to be conscious of the fact we are angry and to investigate whether it is really worthwhile.

Question: It is hard to break patterns of emotions sometimes.

Lama Govinda: Yes, the moment a thing becomes a pattern, it becomes difficult. But you can break a pattern by becoming conscious of that pattern and by discriminating. If you see things clearly and understand them, then generally you'll already be free of them. In our relationship with other human beings, I think we are mostly angry at others because we do not understand their attitudes. When we can put ourselves into the attitude of another person, very often, though we perhaps may not share the idea, we can then understand them.

Question: Sometimes people refer to your karma as your destiny ...

Lama Govinda: No, karma is not destiny. Destiny means predestination, and in Buddhism we do not believe in predestination. We believe that karma is only character. Every deed adds to your character, forms your character in a way. Good deeds make you better, bad deeds make you worse. That means you improve your character by every good deed, and you diminish your character by any mean deed. Therefore, in the uppermost sense, karma is not different from character.

Notes

EDITOR'S NOTE: Lama Govinda traveled extensively and spent long months, even years, in remote places. He was not well funded or independently wealthy. Nor were as many important texts available in wide book distribution as they are today. Furthermore, Lama Govinda toiled in the Industrial Age, not the Information Age. He could not go wireless at a Starbucks in Katmandu and Google a reference. But he was multilingual, erudite, and deeply immersed in the art, literature, and philosophy of both the East and the West. He also had an encyclopedic memory. In the course of editing this collection of writings, there were numerous instances in which Govinda quoted something either from memory or from his own translation of a text unavailable in English. Wherever possible, if Govinda's own references were incomplete, an appropriate source has been provided. The endnotes for the Introduction are, of course, the editor's. But the endnotes for Chapters 1 through 6 are Govinda's, unless enclosed within brackets. Those within brackets are notes that have been completed or revised by the editor.

INTRODUCTION

1. Lama Govinda, *The Way of the White Clouds* (Woodstock, NY: Overlook Press, 2005), 25.

2. Jane Hope and Borin Van Loon, *Buddha for Beginners* (Duxford: Icon Books, 1994), 155.

3. Rick Fields, *How the Swans Came to the Lake* (Boulder: Shambhala, 1981), 119–29.

4. Nyogen Senzaki, *Like A Dream, Like A Fantasy* (Tokyo: Japan Publications, 1978), 103–4.

5. Lobsang Wangyal, "45 years ago, witness to Dalai Lama's flight did not know history being made," *Agence France Presse,* March 17, 2004.

6. Ken Winkler, *A Thousand Journeys: The Biography of Lama Anagarika Govinda* (London: Vega, 2002), 103–4.

7. Letters from Lama Govinda and Li Gotami, Human Dimensions Institute Archive.

8. Govinda, *Way of the White Clouds*, 11.

9. Huston Smith Notes, Human Dimensions Institute Archive.

10. John Blofeld, *The Wheel of Life* (London: Rider, 1959).

11. Winkler, *A Thousand Journeys*, 9.

12. Ibid., 8.

13. Huston Smith Notes, Human Dimensions Institute Archive.

14. Govinda, *Way of the White Clouds*, xx.

15. Winkler, *A Thousand Journeys*, 19.

16. Govinda, *Way of the White Clouds*, 13.

17. Winkler, *A Thousand Journeys*, 79.

18. Ibid., 91.

19. Govinda, *Way of the White Clouds*, 346.

20. Winkler, *A Thousand Journeys*, 120.

21. Huston Smith Notes, Human Dimensions Institute Archive.

22. Ibid.

23. Ken Winkler, *Pilgrim of Clear Light: The Biography of Dr. Walter Y. Evans-Wentz* (Berkeley: Dawn Fire, 1982).

24. Theosophical Society, San Francisco Lodge Archives.

25. Richard Power, *Great Song: Life and Teachings of Joe and Guin Miller* (Athens, GA: Maypop Books, 1993), 165.

26. Maitland Zane, "The Circling of Mt. Tam on Buddha's Birthday," *San Francisco Chronicle*, April 9, 1969.

27. Theosophical Society, San Francisco Lodge Archives.

28. Ibid.

29. Ibid.

30. Winkler, *A Thousand Journeys*, 154.

31. Govinda, *Way of the White Clouds*, 30.

32. A. F. Price and Wong Mou-lam, *Diamond Sutra & Sutra of Hui-Neng* (Boston: Shambhala, 1990), 53.

33. Govinda, *Way of the White Clouds*, 31.

34. Ibid., 37, 38–39.

35. Ibid., 86–89.

36. Lama Govinda, *Foundations of Tibetan Mysticism* (New York: E. P Dutton and Co., 1960), 24–25.

37. Ibid., 59.

38. Ibid., 89.

39. Ibid., 190.

40. Lama Anagarika Govinda, *Psycho-Cosmic Symbolism of the Buddhist Stupa* (Berkeley: Dharma Publishing, 1976), 78.

41. Ibid., 84–85.

42. Lama Govinda, *Creative Meditation and Multi-Dimensional Consciousness* (Wheaton, IL: Theosophical Publishing House, Quest Books, 1976), 50–51.

43. Ibid., 52.

44. Ibid., 53.

45. Ibid.

46. Huston Smith Notes, Human Dimensions Institute Archive.

47. Lama Anagarika Govinda, *The Inner Structure of the I CHING* (Tokyo: Wheelwright/Weatherhill, 1981), 10.

48. Kyle Jarrard, "A Monk's Meditation on the Pursuit of Happiness," *International Herald Tribune*, June 30, 2006.

49. Anthony Barnes, "The Happiest Man in the World?" *The Independent*, March 12, 2007.

1. FROM THERAVADA TO ZEN

1. [Bikkhu Bodhi, *The Connected Discourses of the Buddha: A Translation of the Samyutta Nikāya* (Boston: Wisdom Publications, 2002) 537.]
2. [*Milinda Panha*, circa 100 BCE, literally "Questions of Milinda," included in the Pali canon.]
3. [Max F. Muller, trans., *Sacred Books of the East*, Vol. XII (New York: Charles Scribner's Sons, 1901); H. Saddhatissa, *Sutta-Nipāta* (London: Routledge Curzon, 1995).]
4. [D. T. Suzuki, *Lankavatara Sutra* (London: Routledge and Kegan Paul, 1966).]
5. [A. F. Price and Wong Mou-lam, *Diamond Sutra & Sutra of Hui-Neng* (Boston: Shambhala, 1990), 70.]
6. [Max F. Muller, trans., *Sacred Books of the East*, Vol. XV (Oxford, 1884), 242.]
7. [Price, and Mou-lam, *Diamond Sutra*, (Boston: Shambhala, 1990), 72.]
8. [Ibid., xx.]

2. *THE ACT OF WILL* AND ITS ROLE IN THE PRACTICE OF MEDITATION

1. Dr. Roberto Assagioli, *The Act of Will* (New York: Viking Press, 1973), 10.
2. Ibid., 10.
3. Ibid., 21.
4. Ibid., 5–6.
5. Ibid.
6. Ibid., 113.
7. Jacob Bronowski, "The Reach of Imagination." [In Jacob Bronowski, *A Sense of the Future: Essays in Natural Science* (Cambridge, MA: MIT Press, 1978).]
8. Assagioli, *The Act of Will*, 51, 52, 56.
9. Ibid., 194.

3. TEILHARD DE CHARDIN IN
THE MIRROR OF EASTERN THOUGHT

1. Lama Anagarika Govinda, *Creative Meditation and Multi-Dimensional Consciousness* (Wheaton, IL: Theosophical Publishing House, Quest Books, 1976).

2. Edward W. Sinnott, *The Biology of the Spirit* (New York: Viking Press, 1955), 47.

3 Ibid., 61.

4. Lama Anagarika Govinda, *The Psychological Attitude of Early Buddhist Philosophy* (London: Rider and Company, 1961).

5. Sinnott, *Biology of the Spirit*, 71.

6. Ibid., 115.

7. Ibid., 52.

8. Pierre Teilhard de Chardin, *Hymn of The Universe*, trans. Norman Denny (London: Collins, 1965), 19.

9. Ibid., 20.

10. Ibid.

11. Teilhard de Chardin, *Hymn of The Universe*, 27.

12. Ibid., 27, 28.

13. Rainer Maria Rilke, *Selected Works* (London: Hogart Press, 1960), 2:186–87.

14. Teilhard de Chardin, *Hymn of The Universe* (Collins, 1965), 69.

15. Jean Gebser, *Ursprung und Gegenwart* (Stuttgart: Deutsche Verlagsanstalt, 1966), 2:405.

16. Teilhard de Chardin, *Hymn of The Universe*, 69, 77–78, 113.

17. Ibid., 29.

18. Ibid., 33.

19. Sinnott, *Biology of the Spirit*, 161–62.

20. Medard Boss, *Indienfahrt Eines Psychiaters* (Pfullingen, Germany: Günther Neske, 1959), 19.

21. Gebser, *Ursprung und Gegenwart*, 1:327.

22. Alan Watts, *The Supreme Identity* (New York: Pantheon, 1959), 56.

23. Boss, *Indienfahrt Eines Psychiaters.*

24. Sinnott, *Biology of the Spirit*, 88, 90.

25. Teilhard de Chardin, *The Future of Man*, trans. Norman Denny (London: Collins, 1964), 91.

26. Ibid., 122, 30.

27. Ibid., 92.

28. Ibid., 80.

4. Drugs and Meditation

1. Jean Gebser, *Ursprung und Gegenwart* (Stuttgart: Deutsche Verlagsanstalt, 1966), 1:56.

2. [*Goethe's Faust*, trans. Walter Kaufmann (New York: Anchor Books, 1990), 114.]

3. Karlfried Graf Von Dürckheim, *Hara: The Vital Centre of Man* (London: George Allen & Unwin, 1962), 83 (italics mine).

5. Meditation

1. [Although Govinda did not cite a specific text in his reference to Novalis, this passage from *Miscellaneous Observations* (1798) captures the sentiment: "The imagination places the world of the future either far above us, or far below, or in a relation of metempsychosis to ourselves. We dream of traveling through the universe— but is not the universe within ourselves? The depths of our spirit are unknown to us—the mysterious way leads inwards. · Eternity with its worlds—the past and future—is in ourselves or nowhere. The external world is the world of shadows—it throws its shadow into the realm of light. At present this realm certainly seems to us so dark inside, lonely, shapeless. But how entirely different it will seem to us—when this gloom is past, and the body of shadows has moved away. We will experience greater enjoyment than ever, for our spirit has been deprived."]

2. Charles Luk, trans., *Surangama Sutra* (Rider and Company, 1966), 118–21.
3. Edward W. Sinnott, *The Biology of the Spirit* (New York: Viking Press, 1955), 64, 66.
4. Jacquetta Hawkes, "An Aside on Consciousness," in *The Human Spirit*, ed. Whit Burnett (London: George Allen & Unwin, 1960).
5. Jalal ad-Din [Rumi], trans. H. L. Myers.
6. Karlfried Graf Von Dürckheim, *Hara: The Vital Centre of Man* (London: George Allen & Unwin, 1962), 158–59.
7. Ibid., 18.

6. A New Way to Look at the I Ching

1. [Richard Wilhelm, *I Ching or The Book of Changes* (New York: Pantheon Books, Bollingen Series, 1950), 1:292.]
2. [Ibid., xl–xli.]
3. [Ibid., 317.]
4. [Ibid., 134–35.]

Selected Bibliography
Life and Work of Lama Govinda

EDITOR'S NOTE: By his own account, Lama Govinda authored over thirty books. This selected bibliography includes his major works, as well as texts of other authors relevant to the scope and themes of this collection. The titles selected reflect both the work of Govinda's contemporaries and more recent contributions from worthy sources.

LAMA GOVINDA AND LI GOTAMI

Gotami, Li, and Lama Anagarika Govinda. *Tibet in Pictures: Text and Photos.* Berkeley: Dharma Publishing, 1980.

Govinda, Lama Anagarika. *Creative Meditation and Multi-Dimensional Consciousness.* Wheaton, IL: Theosophical Publishing House, Quest Books, 1976.

———. *Foundations of Tibetan Mysticism.* New York: E. P. Dutton and Company, 1960.

———. *The Inner Structure of the I CHING.* Tokyo: Wheelwright/ Weatherhill, 1981.

———. *Psycho-Cosmic Symbolism of the Buddhist Stupa.* Berkeley: Dharma Publishing, 1976.

———. *Psychological Attitude of Early Buddhist Philosophy.* London: Rider and Company, 1961.

———. *The Way of the White Clouds.* Woodstock, NY: Overlook Press, 2005.

Winkler, Ken. *A Thousand Journeys: The Biography of Lama Anagarika Govinda*. London: Vega, 2002.

TIBETAN BUDDHISM

Dowman, Keith. *Flight of the Garuda: The Dzogchen Tradition of Tibetan Buddhism*, 2nd ed. Ithaca, NY: Snow Lion Publications, 2003.

———. *Sky Dancer: The Secret Life and Songs of the Lady Yeshe Tsogyel*. Ithaca, NY: Snow Lion Publications, 1996.

Evans-Wentz, W. Y. *Tibetan Book of the Dead*, 2nd ed. London: Oxford University Press, 2000.

———. *Tibetan Book of the Great Liberation*, 2nd ed. London: Oxford University Press, 2000.

———. *Tibetan Yoga & Secret Doctrine*, 3rd ed. London: Oxford University Press, 2000.

———, ed. *Tibet's Great Yogi Milarepa*. London: Oxford University Press, 2000.

Gyatso, Tenzin (Dalai Lama XIV). *Open Heart: Practicing Compassion in Everyday Life*. New York: Little, Brown and Company, 2002.

———. *Wisdom of Forgiveness*. New York: Penguin Group (USA), 2005.

Khyentse, Dilgo, *Enlightened Courage: An Explanation of Atisha's Seven Point Mind Training*. Ithaca, NY: Snow Lion Publications, 1993.

———. *Heart Treasure of the Enlightened Ones*. Boston: Shambhala, 1992.

Patrul Rinpoche. *The Words of My Perfect Master*. San Francisco: Harper Collins, 1994.

Rabjam, Longchen. *The Precious Treasury of the Basic Space of Phenomena*. Junction City, CA: Padma Publishing, 2001.

———. *The Precious Treasury of the Way of Abiding*. Junction City, CA: Padma Publishing, 1998.

Ricard, Matthieu. *Happiness: A Guide to Developing Life's Most Important Skill*. New York: Little, Brown & Company, 2007.

Ricard, Matthieu, and Trinh Xuan Thuan. *The Quantum and the Lotus: A Journey to the Frontiers Where Science and Buddhism Meet.* New York: Crown Publishing, 2004.

Thurman, Robert A.F. *Inner Revolution.* New York: Riverhead, 1999.

———. *The Jewel Tree of Tibet: The Enlightenment Engine of Tibetan Buddhism.* New York: The Free Press, 2006.

THERAVADA BUDDHISM

Bhikku, Buddhadasa. *Heartwood of the Bodhi Tree: The Buddha's Teachings on Voidness.* Boston: Wisdom Publications, 1994.

Bodhi, Bikkhu. *The Connected Discourses of the Buddha: A Translation of the Samyutta Nikāya.* Boston: Wisdom Publications, 2002, pp. 537–540.

Sircar, Rina. *Psycho-Ethical Aspects of the Abhidharma.* Lanham, MD: University Press of America, 1999.

Teich, Anne. *Blooming in the Desert: Favorite Teachings of the Wildflower Monk Taungpulu Sayadaw.* Berkeley: North Atlantic Books, 1996.

CH'AN AND ZEN

Blofeld, John. *Zen Teachings of Huang Po.* Boston: Shambhala, 1994.

Gilbert, Don. *Jellyfish Bones.* Nevada City, CA: Blue Dolphin Publishing, 1980.

———. *The Upside Down Circle.* Nevada City, CA: Blue Dolphin Publishing, 1998.

Price, A. F., and Wong Mou-lam. *Diamond Sutra & Sutra of Hui-Neng.* Boston: Shambhala, 1990.

Reps, Paul and Nyogen Senzaki. *Zen Flesh, Zen Bones.* London: Penguin Books, 2000.

Suzuki, Shunryu, *Zen Mind, Beginner's Mind.* Boston: Shambhala, 2000.

I Ching

Wei, Henry. *The Authentic I-Ching*. Hollywood: Newcastle Publishing, 1987.

Wilhelm, Richard, trans. *The I Ching or Book of Changes*, 2 vols. Bollingen Series. New York: Pantheon Books, 1950.

Relevant History and Biography

David-Neel, Alexandra. *Magic and Mystery in Tibet*. New York: Dover, 1971.

Fields, Rick. *How The Swans Came to The Lake: A Narrative History of Buddhism in America*. Boulder: Shambhala, 1981.

Harrer, Heinrich. *Seven Years in Tibet*. Los Angeles: Tarcher, 1997.

King, Ursula. *Spirit of Fire: The Life and Vision of Teilhard de Chardin*. Orbis, 1998.

Paine, Jeffrey. *Re-Enchantment: Tibetan Buddhism Comes to the West*. New York: W. W. Norton and Company, 2004.

Power, Richard. *Great Song: Life and Teachings of Joe and Guin Miller*. Athens, GA: Maypop, 1993.

Ricard, Matthieu. *Journey to Enlightenment: The Life and World of Khyentse Rinpoche, Spiritual Teacher From Tibet*. New York: Aperture, 1996.

Senzaki, Nyogen. *Like A Dream, Like A Fantasy*. Tokyo: Japan Publications, 1978.

Smith, Huston. *Forgotten Truth: The Common Vision of the World's Great Religions*. San Francisco: Harper San Francisco, 1992.

———. *The Religions of Man*. New York: Harper & Row, 1965.

Winkler, Ken. *Pilgrim of Clear Light: The Biography of Dr. Walter Y. Evans-Wentz*. Berkeley: Dawn Fire, 1982.

Watts, Alan, *In My Own Way: An Autobiography, 1915–1965*. New York: Vintage, 1973.

Index

concentration, 124

"cosmic play," 126

Creative Meditation and Multi-Dimensional Consciousness, xxxix, xlv–xlvii, lii

Dalai Lama, xviii, xix, xxi

Darwin, 44, 58–59

David-Neel, Alexandra, xviii, xxxii, xxxiii

de Chardin, Teilhard, li, liv–lv, 33–34, 46–47, 49–50, 54, 56–58, 61–62, 64, 66–67

Dharma

attached to, 120

hearing, 43

overcomes distinctions, xlix

planetary force, xvii

theory, 3

universal law, 23–24

wheel of, xvii, xix

without understanding, 126

Dharma chanda, 120

Dharmakāya, xxxvi, 52, 130

dhyāna mudra, 102

Dhyāna school (sudden enlightenment), 13

Digha-Nikāya, 96

Eightfold Path, 4

ESP, xxiii

Eucharistic ideas, 46

Evans-Wentz, W. Y., xviii, xix, xxxii, xxxv, xxxviii

Foundations of Tibetan Mysticism, xxxiv, xxxix, xliii–xliv, 65, 118

Four Noble Truths, 4

Francis, Saint, 49, 55, 136

Freud, Sigmund, l, 60

Gandhi, Indira, xxix

Gebser, Jean, 36–37, 54–55, 61, 70

Ghose, Sri Aurobindo, 35

Ginsberg, Allen, xxxiv

Goethe, Wolfgang, 41, 71

Gospel of St. John, 52

Gotami, Li

chronicled journey to Tsaparang, xxx

descent into Langchen-Khambab, xx

Illustrated Weekly of India, xxx

male and female archetypes, lviii

married, xxx

name at birth, xxix

Parkinson's disease, xxxviii

photographic work, xxx

returned to India, xxxix

Tibet in Pictures, xxx

Govinda, Lama

arrival in Colombo, xxvii

biography of, xxi

death, xvi, xxxix

internment, xxix

male and female archetypes, lviii

married, xxx

meaning of "Anagarika Govinda," xxvii–xxviii

Nirmāṇakāya, xxxvi, 51, 130

nirvana, 132

Novalis, 80, 144n1 (chap. 5)

Nyingma Institute, xxxviii

Olcott, H. S., xviii

Om Hari Krishna Om, 119

Oṁ Maṇi Padme Hūṁ, xxxvii, xliii–
xliv, li, 47, 118

padmāsana, 102

paradox, 14

Petit, Rati, xxix

power, 21

prajna, 19

Prajnaparamita-hridaya, 9

prāṇa, 94, 99, 101

prāṇayama, 98

pratītya-samutpāda, 7

*Psycho-Cosmic Symbolism of the
Buddhist Stupa*, xxxix, xliv–xlv

*Psychological Attitude of Early Buddhist
Philosophy*, xxviii, 43

psychosynthesis, 29, 31

Rand, Yvonne, xv

Ricard, Matthieu, lvi–lvii

Rilke, Ranier Maria, 53–54

Rindge, Jeanne, xv

Roerich, Nicholas, xviii, lviii

Rumi, 93

samadhi, xix, 132

Samboghakāya, xxxvi, 51, 130

samsara, 71

samyak-sambodhi, 18

Śāntideva, 48–49

Shaku, Soyen, xviii, xx

Shakyamuni, xvii, 57

Shapiro, Bob, xx

Shuo Kua, 106

Siddhartha, xxvii–xxviii, 57

Sincar, Rina, xviii

Sinnott, Edmund W., 42, 58, 63

Sixth Patriarch, 14–17, 19

Smith, Huston, xxii, xxiv, xxvi, xxxiii,
xxxiv, xlvii, lvii

śūnyam, 8

śūnyatā, xlix, 8, 82–83, 135

Surangama Sutra, 55, 84

Sutta-Nipaāa, 9

Suzuki, D. T., 27, 84

Synder, Gary, xxxiv

Tao, 107

Tarthang Tulku, xxxviii

Tathagata, 11

theory of relativity, 4

Theravada Buddhism

canon, 2

only authentic form of, 1

*Thousand Journeys, A: The Biography
of Lama Anagarika Govinda*, xxi

Thurman, Robert, xiii, xxi

Tomo Geshe Rinpoche, xxix, xxxiv

Trungpa, Chögyam, xviii

Quest Books

encourages open-minded inquiry into
world religions, philosophy, science, and the arts
in order to understand the wisdom of the ages,
respect the unity of all life, and help people explore
individual spiritual self-transformation.

Its publications are generously supported by
The Kern Foundation,
a trust committed to Theosophical education.

Quest Books is the imprint of
the Theosophical Publishing House,
a division of the Theosophical Society in America.
For information about programs, literature,
on-line study, membership benefits, and international centers,
see www.theosophical.org
or call 800-669-1571 or (outside the U.S.) 630-668-1571.

To order books or a complete Quest catalog,
call 800-669-9425 or (outside the U.S.) 630-665-0130.

Related Quest Titles

The Illustrated Encyclopedia of Buddhist Wisdom,
by Gill Farrer-Halls

Mother of the Buddhas, by Lex Hixon

The Opening of the Wisdom-Eye,
by the Fourteenth Dalai Lama

Tibetan Healing, by Peter Fenton

The World of the Dalai Lama, by Gill Farrer-Halls

To order books or a complete Quest catalog,
call 800-669-9425 or (outside the U.S.) 630-665-0130.

Praise for Richard Power's

The Lost Teachings of Lama Govinda

"Fascinating! The many admirers of Lama Govinda will be grateful to Richard Power for bringing together the Lama's lost teachings. I had the privilege of meeting Lama Govinda and his wife, Li Gotami, in their beautiful Kesar Devi Ashram in the lower Himalayas in the early summer of 1966 when he was going through the galley proofs of his well-known book *The Way of White Clouds* and she was preparing a book of photographs from their trip to Tibet.

Lama Govinda gave me a copy of the proofs to read overnight before coming to see him the next day. I found the text exhilarating and him wise, a pioneer of the human spirit. His life and writings did not present any cheap or easy synthesis of the divergent psychological and spiritual tendencies of the East and the West, but held them in a creative and fruitful tension."

—Ravi Ravindra, author, *Centered Self without Being Self-Centered* and *Science and the Sacred*

Praise for Richard Power's

The Lost Teachings of Lama Govinda

"Lama Anagarika Govinda was one of the pioneers of Tibetan and Buddhist studies in the West. His writings in this volume complement his important books, show the depth and range of his mind, and give a good sense of how he was in person. I recommend it for those wishing to understand the deeper history of the introduction of Tibetan Buddhism in the West."
—Robert A. F. Thurman, Professor of Indo-Tibetan Buddhist Studies in the Department of Religion, Columbia University; cofounder and current president, Tibet House U.S., New York City; author of *The Tibetan Book of the Dead.*

"The modern Western perspective that Lama Govinda brings to this study of Vajrayana Buddhism imbues it with a rare clarity and vigor— and is especially valuable for anyone seeking to explore the deeper reaches of Buddhist 'whole body' meditation. I found it richly rewarding."
—Victoria LePage, author, *Shambhala: The Fascinating Truth behind the Myth of Shangri-la*

"Lama Govinda's work has changed my life and work. I find in him the rarest fusion of majestic realization, philosophical depth, and exquisite literary ability. Anyone interested in mysticism and its role in our current crisis will find this brilliant book both useful and profoundly inspiring."
—Andrew Harvey, author, *The Direct Path* and *Dialogues with a Modern Mystic*